What people are say

Speculative Annihi.

Too often speculative philosophies forget that the thought of extinction invariably opens onto the extinction of thought – and that this may very well be what thinking is. Rosen's book takes up this insight and extends it, levelling up Levinas beyond the staid traditions of phenomenology and ethics into which his work is so often pigeonholed. In the process, Rosen discovers an archaeology that is more philosophical than speculative philosophy, an archae-ontology that is the alpha and omega of the species that thinks itself as a species.
Eugene Thacker, author of *In The Dust of This Planet*

While there is no shortage of engagements with Speculative Realism and its varied effects, Rosen takes up the strange diachronic form of Quentin Meillassoux's temporality in a fascinating manner. Emphasizing the thinkability of extinction through these temporal divergences, Rosen investigates the peculiarities of archaeology and proto-human life and ends with a novel engagement with Levinas and the inevitable but unavoidable encounter with a putrefied otherness.
Ben Woodard, author of *On an Ungrounded Earth* and *Slime Dynamics*

Rosen's *Speculative Annihilationism* brilliantly poses difficult questions — about the facticity of extinction, about being without thought — and dares to answer them. We should thank him for showing us the way in such clear, concise language, for peeling back the bruised veil and rendering the utterances of the abyss intelligible. Here now we can grasp extinction for what it really is — not possibility, but inevitability.
David Peak, author of *The Spectacle of the Void*

Speculative Annihilationism attempts something with archaeology that will seem absurd to so many working in the field: the decoupling of the archaeologist's thinking from the artifacts that archaeology unearths. But in light of Quentin Meillassoux's groundbreaking work of speculative materialism in *After Finitude* and related maneuvers conducted in contemporary speculative metaphysics, we can identify Rosen's project for what it is: a risky work of noncorrelationist archaeology, a speculative thinking that attempts to extricate the past from history—to tear the past out of time itself—and in the attempt finds decay, horror, and nihilism at its center. In other words, it aims to think the Absolute at the peril of thought itself, and it's not afraid to do so.

Tom Sparrow, Assistant Professor of Philosophy, Slippery Rock University, USA

Speculative Annihilationism

The Intersection of Archaeology and Extinction

Speculative Annihilationism

The Intersection of Archaeology and Extinction

Matt Rosen

Winchester, UK
Washington, USA

First published by Zero Books, 2019
Zero Books is an imprint of John Hunt Publishing Ltd., No. 3 East St., Alresford,
Hampshire SO24 9EE, UK
office1@jhpbooks.net
www.johnhuntpublishing.com
www.zero-books.net

For distributor details and how to order please visit the 'Ordering' section on our website.

ISBN: 978 1 78904 147 7
978 1 78904 148 4 (ebook)
Library of Congress Control Number: 2018943951

A CIP catalogue record for this book is available from the British Library.

Design: Stuart Davies

UK: Printed and bound by CPI Group (UK) Ltd, Croydon, CR0 4YY
US: Printed and bound by Thomson Shore, 7300 West Joy Road, Dexter, MI 48130

We operate a distinctive and ethical publishing philosophy in
all areas of our business, from our global network of authors to
production and worldwide distribution.

Contents

Preface

Archaeology matters because extinction matters. We find ourselves ensnared, intertwined, and entangled in an age of extinctions which presents us with theoretical and philosophical opportunities of paramount importance. As of yet, theory has not caught up, but rather lags behind the exigencies of the Holocene. Our philosophy asks "is science true?" instead of "what is science doing?" Our ontology foregrounds stasis and permanence, relegating talk of decay, degeneration, putrefaction, death, extinction, and the like to the postulatory back-burner.

Archaeology, the praxis of exhumation and thus the praxis of extinction-analysis, depends on a set of theoretic beliefs, presuppositions, and claims that are similarly inadequate in regard to addressing the exigencies of our age. Archaeological theoretic approaches of a post-processual, cultural-historical, or post-modernist bent are not equipped to grant issues of extinction the attentiveness and diligent contemplation that they are warranted. These theoretic approaches tend to conjure the incubi of correlationism, philosophies of access, philosophies of human finitude, and — in general — the Kantian and post-Kantian conceit that being and thought are inseparably correlated such that neither can be understood independently and that the human is in some sort of privileged position vis-à-vis other entities. My central task in this text, then, will be to suggest an alternative ontological and theoretic approach to archaeology in light of the implications of our entanglement in this present age of extinctions.

It should be said, straightaway, that this text can serve as only a précis, and that the suggestions made here do little more than skim the surface of a plethora of areas of inquiry worthy of much further consideration. This book is the product of a putrefied-thought: following Levinas — whose ethics as ontology it seeks to engage, darken, and make profane — it will not prioritize rational argumentation and answers, but will rather emphasize images and questions. It will attempt to complexify rather than solve, provoke rather than allay, disorient rather than situate ad nauseam, and engage in fragmentary speculation rather than holistic teleology. The Kantian and post-Kantian correlationist conceit has been ingrained in such a way that we must be shaken out of it. This text thus aims both for the neatness of utmost clarity and the perplexity of unrestrained theory.

Where possible, I have taken every effort to explain the jargon used and to locate the reader in a wider theoretic context. This has not been unconditionally possible, as a full elaboration of the universe of discourse discussed would needlessly convolute this slender volume.

It is my hope that this text can act as a small admonition against a mélange of anthropomorphisms, correlationisms, philosophies of access, philosophies of human finitude, idealisms, contextualisms, and postmodernisms which all too often characterize the way in which we think about science, reason, and our place in the cosmos — a place that theory frequently seems to overstate. My contention herein will be that we really can know about *what is* through scientific praxis reframed as speculation, and that what we discover in what is, its is-ness, is a horror reality which our age of extinctions brings to the fore. The Holocene calls for an ontological reorientation apropos of the way in which we conceptualize the relation between ourselves, other species, and the facticity of extinction. This reorientation is towards a mad, black Levinasianism — towards speculative annihiliationism.

Acknowledgments

Philosophy is the labor of many minds and this book is no exception. First, a great deal of gratitude is owed to all of the editorial staff at Zer0 Books and John Hunt Publishing, this text would not exist in its present state without their countless hours of work and dedication.

This book stands upon the groundwork laid by innumerable thinkers, theorists, and philosophers; any acknowledgment is thus bound to leave out a considerable number of them. That being said, I am indebted — in particular — to the work of Emmanuel Levinas. The ideas herein should be read as elaborations or derivations of his inexhaustible ouevre. I am indebted, as well, to the groundbreaking work of Quentin Meillassoux, Reza Negarestani, Eugene Thacker, Nick Land, Gilles Deleuze and Félix Guattari, Martin Heidegger, Ray Brassier, David Peak, and Ben Woodard.

To MH, whose illuminative critiques encouraged me to clarify and deepen my thought. To EW, whose support, assistance, and thoughtful listening were absolutely indispensable and crucial to this book's development. To JL, for making philosophy fresh and exciting, and for encouraging both careful contemplation and unbridled speculation. To MM, for instilling in me a love of thought. To my sister, Talia, for years of bearing with me.

And, most of all, I owe an irredeemable debt of gratitude to my parents, who taught me to question everything, to pursue my passions, to never accept quick or easy answers, and to embrace the virtues of idiosyncrasy.

Introduction: Lomekwi 3

In July 2011, a team of archaeologists led by Sonia Harmand and Jason Lewis made a wrong turn near Lake Turkana, in Kenya, near a site where fossils of *Kenyanthropus platyops* had previously been found. That wrong turn proved fateful: the team ended up in a previously unexplored region and discovered artifacts which they dated to approximately 3.3 million years ago, naming the site "Lomekwi 3."[1]

At Lomekwi 3, the archaeologists unearthed about 20 well-preserved artifacts, including flakes, anvils, and other tools. The stratigraphic position of the artifacts allowed the team to date them to 3.3 million years ago, predating our own genus, *Homo*, by about 500,000 years. This suggests that the artifacts were used by another genus of hominins, perhaps *Australopithecus* or *Kenyanthropus*. For our purposes, the artifact-makers of Lomekwi 3 will simply be called *Australopithecus*. When this term is used, it refers specifically to that species which made and used the artifacts discovered at Lomekwi 3.

Australopithecus evolved in Africa around 4 million years ago, spread across the continent for about 2 million years, and then *became extinct* 2 million years ago. It is important to note that Lomekwi 3 is unique, differing from other archaeological discoveries in a substantial way: Australopithecus is extinct and left no easily discernible cultural or historical record. This leaves us in a place of considerable epistemic indetermination vis-à-vis, for instance, the discovery of Chinese, Greek, or Roman artifacts.

1

Quasi-Australopithecus

1.1 Archaeological theoretic approaches

The discovery of artifacts at Lomekwi 3 and the epistemic indetermination that ensued are problematic for current archaeological theoretic approaches, particularly those of a post-processual, cultural-historical, or post-modernist bent. These archaeological theoretic approaches each engage in varieties of anthropomorphic interpretation.

Post-processual archaeology, while multifaceted, tends to emphasize the subjective nature of archaeological interpretation. It was pioneered by archaeologists in the United Kingdom in the 1970s and 1980s as a reaction to processual archaeology, which theorized that the application of the scientific method could result in objective conclusions. For processualists, archaeology could employ evidence to make true claims about past societies.

Post-processual archaeology must be understood in this context, as a reactionary movement against the positivism of processual archaeology. Against positivist claims, post-processual archaeologist Matthew Johnson tells us that "all archaeologists...whether they overtly admit it or not" engage in subjectivism, imposing their own perspective on their interpretations of archaeological evidence.[2]

Johnson tells us that "we can never confront theory and data; instead, we see data through a cloud of theory."[3] Influenced by Feyerabend's "methodological anarchism," post-processualists such as Johnson view evidence or facts as inherently theory-laden. Compare Johnson's claim with Feyerabend's: "experience arises together with theoretical assumptions, not before them, and an experience without a theory is just as incomprehensible as is (allegedly) a theory without an experience."[4]

For Johnson and Feyerabend, theoretical assumptions must be made before a scientist can go out and "do science" so that the collection of the data is meaningful. A scientist collects data in order to build on or attempt to falsify a theory, not in a vacuum. All scientific data is based on a presupposition of some theory. This theory-ladenness argument questions whether science can be characterized by a distinct methodology; if scientists must presuppose theoretical assumptions prior to conducting science, the scientific methodology begins to blur with methodologies characteristic of what might be considered nonscience or pseudoscience.

Many post-processualists argue that facts should be interpreted with both materialist and idealist theoretical frameworks. Johnson again: "Many postprocessualists claim that we should reject the whole opposition between material and ideal in the first place."[5] While acknowledging that past societies often interpret the world materially, post-processualists also acknowledge that those societies tended to value ideologies and religious traditions. For instance, in regard to the archaeological interpretation of landscapes, Johnson writes: "postprocessualists like to argue that landscapes are always viewed in different ways by different peoples."[6]

Post-processual archaeology stands on two legs: subjectivism and relativism. Archaeological interpretations are deemed subjective, liable to the undue influence of the bias of the archaeologist doing the interpreting. Archaeological objects (particularly cultures) are deemed relative, both distinct from one another and incommensurable with one another. Because an archaeologist cannot escape their relative culture, the subjectivism of interpretation is understood as inescapable. *Cultural-historical archaeology* emphasizes inductive reasoning — along with post-processual archaeology, because facts are seen as theory-laden — and the incommensurability of "material cultures." Unlike the processual archaeology which succeeded it, cultural-historical archaeology employs an inductive rather than hypothetic-deductive method. In this sense, it is post-processual archaeology's precursor.

Cultural-historical archaeology was first developed in Germany and was introduced to the English-speaking world in the 1920s; it continues to influence contemporary archaeological debates. In *Culture History: A Cultural-Historical Approach*, Gary S. Webster writes that cultural-historical archaeology's central feature is its "statements which reveal common notions about the nature of ancient cultures; about their qualities; about how they related to the material record; and thus about how archaeologists might effectively study them."[7] That is, cultural-historical archaeology views archaeological interpretation as dependent on and inextricable from the historical record, from which it draws its claims. Of course, this historical record is in turn inextricable from our own cultural or historical biases. This argument can be understood syllogistically:

1. Archaeological interpretation (A) is dependent on/inextricable from the historical record (B).
2. The historical record (B) is dependent on/inextricable from our cultural biases (C).
3. Archaeological interpretation (A) is dependent on/inextricable from our cultural biases (C).

The conclusion (3) rests on premises 1 and 2. One of the aims of this project is to problematize premise 1 — thereby undermining the conclusion — by suggesting that archaeological interpretation can speculate about extinction (thinking the extinction of thought) and therefore can be excised from the historical record.

Post-modernist archaeology, which follows from post-modernist anthropology, emphasizes opinion and perspective, utilizing cultural relativist frameworks as methods of inquiry. It originated in the 1960s, informed generally by the cultural post-modern movement and more specifically by Kuhn's paradigmatic account of science and by Feyerabend's tour de force, *Against Method*.

Post-modernist archaeology attempts to grant legitimacy to the perspectives or opinions of those cultures being studied. Clifford Geertz, often considered a founder of post-modernist anthropology, writes: "anthropological writings are themselves interpretations, and second and third ones to boot."[8] Again, compare with Feyerabend: "My intention is not to replace one set of general rules by another such set: my intention is, rather, to convince the reader that all *methodologies, even the most obvious ones, have their limits*."[9]

In each of these archaeologies, there is a deep skepticism regarding "scientific claims" and a tendency towards anthropomorphism. A certain methodological, cultural, linguistic, and historical mode is seen as inescapable and, thus, to talk of an extinct species requires us to acknowledge that we cannot escape our own mode. These theoretic approaches tend to problematize the interpretation of evidence in regard to human civilizations, rendering those interpretations subjective and the cultures/people under consideration, relative. The interpretation of evidence in regard to extinct species becomes even more problematic.

For these programs, the question of *what it would be like to be the Australopithecus who made or used these artifacts* is either unintelligible or ill-posed. This question presupposes that we can observe data about the Australopithecus unclouded by theory (contra post-processual archaeology), that we can deduce claims without a historical record in place (contra cultural-historical archaeology), and that we can go beyond interpretations which are bound to a culture about which we can know nothing (contra post-modernist archaeology).

For the post-processual archaeologist, our theoretic frameworks seem alien when applied to other human peoples, let alone Australopithecus. With archaeological interpretations about humans, our inescapable mode is noticeable but can often be adequately addressed by considering the opinions or perspectives of a people's contemporary descendants or by detailing and setting aside assumptions that the archaeologist's context may entail. With archaeological interpretations about Australopithecus, our inescapable mode seems glaring. We are not just dealing with another culture or historical context, but with another species and genus. Considering the opinions of a contemporary Australopithecus is evidently impossible and setting aside certain assumptions becomes an act not only of cultural escape but of anti-speciesism.

Instead of asking *what it would be like to be the Australopithecus who made or used these artifacts*, we are left with the question of *what it would be like for a human (and a human in our time and in our culture and with our scientific method, etc.) to imagine being the Australopithecus who made or used these artifacts*. These are two very different questions.

The former asks about the phenomenal experience of Australopithecus in regard to the making or usage of the artifacts, while the latter asks about the phenomenal experience of an archaeologist imagining Australopithecus in contextual (viz., human, cultural, linguistic) terms which are unavoidable and inescapable. The former purports to speak of truth, while the latter purports to speak only of interpretation.

The latter question can be regarded as essentially Nietzschean. In *Will to Power*, Nietzsche writes: "No, facts is precisely what there is not, only interpretations."[10] This view is the result of Nietzsche's nihilism in which aesthetic preference replaces truth. In *Nihil Unbound*, Ray Brassier elaborates on this view: "according to Nietzsche, nihilism reaches its apogee in the pivotal moment when truth, hitherto the supreme value, turns against itself — for it is "truthfulness" itself that calls the value of "truth" into question, thereby subverting all known and knowable values..."[11] Against this view, I quote Brassier at length:

> Like Nietzsche, I think nihilism is a consequence of the "will to truth." *But unlike Nietzsche, I do not think nihilism culminates in the claim that there is no truth.* Nietzsche conflated truth with meaning, and concluded that since the latter is always a result of human artifice, the former is nothing but a matter of convention. However, once truth is dismissed, all that remains is the difference between empowering and disempowering fictions, where "life" is the fundamental source of empowerment and the ultimate arbiter of the difference between life-enhancing and life-depreciating fictions. Since the abandonment of truth undermines the reason for relinquishing illusion, it ends up licensing the concoction of further fictional narratives, the only requirement for which is that they prove to be "life-enhancing". *I consider myself a nihilist precisely to the extent that I refuse this Nietzschean solution and continue to believe in the difference between truth and falsity, reality and appearance. In other words, I am a nihilist precisely because I still believe in truth,* unlike those whose triumph over nihilism is won at the cost of sacrificing truth.[12]

Even if our scientific view of the world entails a nihilism in which tales of meaning are taken as fictive and purpose is thought of as an old-fashioned myth, truth can remain intact. The Nietzschean solution is one solution — it is the solution that many contemporary archaeological theoretic approaches assume — but it is by no means the only conceivable solution.

The question of what it would be like for a human (and a human in our time and in our culture and with our scientific method, etc.) to imagine being the Australopithecus who made or used the artifacts discovered at Lomekwi 3 ties being to thought and the real to the phenomenal. This is symptomatic of what Meillassoux critiques as "correlationism" in *After Finitude*. He defines correlationism as "the idea according to which we only ever have access to the correlation between thinking and being, and never to either term considered apart from the other."[13] For Meillassoux, correlationism has been at the center of philosophical thought since Kant. Kant makes two epistemological claims which are relevant to understanding both the Kantian correlation and post-Kantian correlationist philosophies:

1. Things conform to the mental and not vice versa. For Kant, the mental does not only interpret or make sense of the real, but actualizes itself within it, giving it structure.
2. The real (distinct from us) is beyond an insurmountable epistemic wall. We can only know the real as it appears to us phenomenally, i.e., we can only know the appearances of things. It is therefore the rational course of action to profess agnosticism about the state of the real.

Plenty of philosophers after Kant have not accepted his epistemology in its entirety, yet their philosophies remain strains of the correlationist disease. For Wittgenstein and Derrida, being and language are correlated, i.e., one can only have access to being as being-and-language or language as language-and-being. For Foucault, being is correlated with power. These philosophies share a commonality: the real *in-itself* is inaccessible.

Correlationism, following Meillassoux, can be formulated as follows: the statement "z *is*" means "z *is the correlate of thinking-z*." Thinking-z, or z-as-it-appears to me, is the only possibility for access; this is why correlationist philosophies are also termed "philosophies of access." The correlation rather than each element (thought distinct from being) is the only thing that is accessible, and to the extent that accessible here means accessible by humans, philosophies of access are inherently anthropocentric. Truth becomes truth-for-us (anthropocentric truth) and truth-for-us *just is* interpretation. We thus arrive back at the Nietzschean solution.

Meillassoux writes: "contemporary philosophy has lost...the *absolute* outside of pre-critical thinkers: that outside which was not relative to us, and which was given as indifferent to its own givenness to be what it is, existing in-itself regardless of whether we are thinking of it or not; that outside which thought could explore with the legitimate feeling of being on foreign territory – of being entirely elsewhere."[14] Similarly, contemporary archaeological theoretic approaches engage in correlationist methods of interpretation — the "outside" is always relative to the archaeologist's mode, culture, or method. The truths of Australopithecus or Lomekwi 3 or extinction must be thought as truths-for-us — as interpretations and nothing besides.

1.2 The resurrection of Australopithecus

In order to ask whether archaeology can decouple being from thought and escape the correlation, let's pose a question: what are we doing when we anthropomorphize an extinct species? That is, what does it mean to ask — as correlationist archaeologies must — what it would be like to be a human imagining what it would be like to be the Australopithecus who made or used the artifacts? What does the construction of this question do to the Australopithecus?

This question performs a resurrection of the Australopithecus *qua* human. Meillassoux again: "Empirical science is today capable of producing statements about events anterior to the advent of life as well as consciousness. These statements consist in the dating of 'objects' that are sometimes older than any form of life on earth."[15] Empirical science (archaeology) is also capable of producing statements about extinct species. In the case of Australopithecus, the species is "anterior to the advent" of human life, thought, and consciousness. Thinking Australopithecus must mean thinking prior to human thought. Correlationisms, though, tell us that thinking "z" (thinking Australopithecus) means thinking "z as the correlate of how z appears to me" (Australopithecus as it appears to me). Australopithecus does not appear to me, *ergo* the only thing that can be done is to resurrect Australopithecus qua human.

Archaeologists wonder about the phenomenal experience of the Australopithecus but are compelled to ask about their own phenomenal experience (human phenomenality) due to the nature of being's correlation with thought. Being cannot be decontextualized. A foregrounding of interpretation and bias — a foregrounding of the archaeologist's mode — necessarily means a backgrounding of fact, truth, and evidence.

Our thinking Australopithecus as the appearance of Australopithecus is a bringing-back-from-extinction, forcing the extinct Australopithecus into a human body or culture or perspective so that it can be examined in human terms. The probable irreversibility of extinction makes this resurrection more problematic than it might otherwise be; e.g., thinking an ancient Egyptian as it appears to me is substantially less troublesome than thinking Australopithecus as it appears to me. At the very least, there are still humans and still Egyptians and, while modern Egyptians may be markedly different from ancient Egyptians, that difference is much more proximate than the difference between a contemporary archaeologist and an Australopithecus.

The resurrection of the Australopithecus as human creates a strange new quasi-Australopithecus, an "Australopithecus-for-us," through which the archaeologist attempts to interpret the artifacts. Consider Johnson once again: "we can never confront theory and data; instead, we see data through a cloud of theory."[16] The quasi-Australopithecus that our anthropomorphic question has built is like Johnson's "cloud of theory": it is the lens through which the data must be examined. The facts (the artifacts discovered at Lomekwi 3) are theory-laden to the degree that the facts are quasi-Australopithecus-laden.

This quasi-Australopithecus-ladenness is problematic because, much like Schrödinger's cat, quasi-Australopithecus is both extinct and not extinct. Schrödinger describes his infamous thought experiment as follows:

> One can even set up quite ridiculous cases. A cat is penned up in a steel chamber, along with the following device (which must be secured against direct interference by the cat): in a Geiger counter, there is a tiny bit of radioactive substance, so small, that perhaps in the course of the hour one of the atoms decays, but also, with equal probability, perhaps none; if it happens, the counter tube discharges and through a relay releases a hammer that shatters a small flask of hydrocyanic acid. If one has left this entire system to itself for an hour, one would say that the cat still lives if meanwhile no atom has decayed. The first atomic decay would have poisoned it. The psi-function of the entire system would express this by having in it the living and dead cat (pardon the expression) mixed or smeared out in equal parts.[17]

For Schrödinger, the livingness of the cat is *indeterminate*: it is unclear whether or not the cat is dead. This indeterminacy is the result of a decoupling of the cat from observation. For the archaeologist operating under post-modernist theoretic presumptions, the livingness of Australopithecus is as indeterminate as the livingness of Schrödinger's cat: it is unclear whether or not or what it would even mean to say that Australopithecus is extinct. This indeterminacy is the result of a coupling of Australopithecus to observation/interpretation. In the archaeological theoretic frameworks discussed, there is no avenue by which human thought can think its own extinction; because these frameworks are correlationist, to think the extinction of Australopithecus is to think our own extinction, and thus to think human thought's extinction. That is, the frameworks have two features which are at odds with one another:

1. Being is inextricable from thought. Therefore, thought cannot think being without thought (the extinction of thought).
2. To think the extinction of Australopithecus is to think the extinction of Australopithecus resurrected as human (i.e., the extinction of humanity). To think the extinction of humanity is to think the extinction of thought.

(1) tells us that thought cannot think the extinction of thought. (2) tells us that thinking the extinction of Australopithecus requires us to think the extinction of thought. This contradiction leads to the conclusion that, for correlationist archaeological theoretic frameworks, the extinction of Australopithecus cannot be thought.

1.3 Empirical extinction

The extinction of Australopithecus is an empirical fact, one about which we can be fairly certain. While I want to be wary of an absolute statement here — it is conceivable that an Australopithecus remains, wandering around the planet in search of others like it — it seems to me that few of us would want to make this claim. Most of us consider it *obvious* that Australopithecus is extinct. Insofar as the Australopithecus can be thought as an Australopithecus, then, *it is extinct*.

Our question, though, performed a resurrection of the Australopithecus as human. Human extinction is not an empirical or observable fact; it is quite hard to imagine in any depth or with any real complexity. Insofar as Australopithecus must be thought as human or within a human mode, then, *it is not extinct*.

Thinking the extinction of Australopithecus seems necessary

for an analysis of the artifacts. Otherwise, the claim *Australopithecus used these artifacts before its extinction* is unthinkable. Suppose that the artifacts discovered at Lomekwi 3 told us something of the way in which Australopithecus became extinct — does it make sense to relegate ourselves, in that instance, to claiming that *the artifacts tell us something of Australopithecus' inconceivable and unthinkable potential extinction*?

Due to the resurrection of Australopithecus as human (i.e., the quasi-Australopithecus), thinking Australopithecus' extinction becomes thinking human extinction. It does not seem to be the case, though, that we can think our own extinction as observable or empirical. The archaeologist then has two recourses: either it is claimed that *we can think our own extinction empirically* or it is claimed that *there is a way to escape the resurrection via anthropomorphism of the Australopithecus as human*.

The first recourse — to think our own extinction empirically — seems untenable. The archaeologist asking what it would be like to be a human imagining what it would be like to be the Australopithecus who made or used the artifacts discovered at Lomekwi 3 is an individual, and one who is not likely to experience human extinction.

For Heidegger, death cannot be known empirically because it is one's "ownmost potentiality-for-being, non-relational, and not to be out-stripped."[18] Let's enumerate each of these conditions in turn and consider the way in which they might bear on human extinction:

1. Death is one's "ownmost potentiality-for-being." That is, death is the thing that makes Dasein individual and unique. Similarly, the way in which a species becomes extinct, the fact of that extinction, is often the defining fact of a species (one need only consider the dodo and the dinosaurs).

2. Death is "non-relational." That is, the death of our own

Dasein cannot be understood through the death of any other Dasein; no one can die for us and we cannot know what it is to die by knowing what it is for someone else to die. Human extinction cannot be understood through the extinction of other species (and we would have a plethora of examples of recent date from which to choose if it could). Knowing how *the dodo* became extinct tells us very little about the way in which *we* will become extinct.

3. Death is "not to be out-stripped." That is, death is not like other endings or like "running out" of anything else. Death is inevitable but indeterminate, we can never be sure how or when it will happen. It is the state of possibility (and inevitability) which is the state of impossibility for Dasein. Extinction, too, is not like other endings. It is inevitable but deeply indeterminate: we cannot know when it will happen or how it will happen and we imagine what it will be like only with great difficulty and in vague detail. The only thing we can say with certainty regarding our own extinction is that it must happen, that the causes which will lead to the end of the possibility for life in our universe have already been set in motion, that it is only a matter of time (see 2.3 for a further discussion of this).

Extinction makes a species distinct and individual (ownmost potentiality-for-being), is not epistemically commensurable between species (non-relational), and is indeterminate but inevitable (not to be out-stripped). These three conditions conspire to disallow the empirical conception of human extinction. *Ergo*, the first recourse fails. We are thus left with the following "scientific" claim: *the Australopithecus-for-us who made or used these artifacts-for-us is extinct-for-us*. With the same legitimacy, we could make nearly any claim that might be true-for-us.

By way of illustration, take note of Feyerabend's defense of

Voodoo as a legitimate practice: "Voodoo...is case in point... everybody uses it as a paradigm of backwardness and confusion. And yet, Voodoo has a firm though still not sufficiently understood material basis, and a study of its manifestations can be used to enrich, and perhaps even revise, our knowledge of physiology."[19] For us, anything can be made legitimate. In fact, Feyerabend makes this absolutely clear: "it will become clear that there is only one principle that can be defended under *all* circumstances and in *all* stages of human development: anything goes."[20]

"Anything goes" — and yet, it does not seem that we should find the claim "*the Australopithecus-for-us who made or used these artifacts-for-us is extinct-for-us*" as satisfying as "*the Australopithecus who made or used the artifacts is extinct.*" The goal of the archaeologist is to render the artifacts intelligible by arriving at a true-for-Australopithecus claim, and "anything goes" will not get us there. Our task, then, will be to find a way to escape the resurrection of the Australopithecus as human.

2

Extinction and Time

2.1 The causal clock

Let's suppose that we have a *causal clock* such that cause and effect occur concurrently. We will use the term "causal clock" to denote a clock which illustrates the causal relation between an event, *a*, and an effect that necessarily and sufficiently follows from it, *b*.[21] "Causal time" will refer to the sort of time that this clock would tell.

Exempli gratia, consider the statement *in "causal time" the birth of a child is concurrent with its death in old age*. This can be said to be true if three conditions are met: (1) the child's birth sufficiently necessitates its eventual death, (2) the child's birth has happened, and (3) we can be reasonably certain that the effect of death follows from birth in all cases, i.e., it is universally true.

(3) is essentially the principle of sufficient reason: the effect of death needs to have a sufficient cause. Meillassoux writes that it is that principle "according to which for every thing, every fact, and every occurrence, there must be a reason why it is thus and so rather than otherwise."[22] For Meillassoux, the principle of sufficient reason is the epitome of dogmatic metaphysics:

If every variant of dogmatic metaphysics is characterized by the thesis that at least one entity is absolutely necessary (the thesis of real necessity), it becomes clear how metaphysics culminates in the thesis according to which every entity is absolutely necessary (the principle of sufficient reason). Conversely, to reject dogmatic metaphysics means to reject all real necessity, and a fortiori to reject the principle of sufficient reason...[23]

It is important to be clear here that causal time does not necessitate (3), i.e., the principle of sufficient reason. Rather, causes and effects that *do* occur concurrently in causal time must abide by (3). There may very well be some effects which do not have "sufficient reason"; these effects do not occur concurrently with their causes in causal time. In the case of the child, though, birth is the cause which necessitates the effect of its death, birth is the necessary and sufficient condition for death, and thus the two occur at the same time on the causal clock.

2.2 An objection considered

Let's consider an objection that might be raised to our notion of causal time: everything has already happened on the causal clock. That is, if all causes and all effects which necessarily and sufficiently follow from those causes happen concurrently in causal time, then everything happens concurrently in causal time. If this is true, causal time collapses causation into nothingness; it is no longer very interesting to say that anything concurred in causal time because everything does.

This objection rests on a contestable presupposition: every effect follows necessarily and sufficiently from the set of all causes. This should seem familiar: it is a simple restatement of the principle of sufficient reason. Meillassoux again: "a principle first formulated by Leibniz, although already at work in Descartes, viz., the principle of sufficient reason, according to which for every thing, every fact, and every occurrence, there must be a reason why it is thus and so rather than otherwise."[24]

There is a misconception at work here. It is assumed that the causal clock necessitates the principle of sufficient reason. This gets it backwards. On the causal clock, those effects which are *sufficiently necessitated* by their causes have already happened. *If* cause and effect concur, then the effect had "sufficient reason." This is not to say, though, that *all* effects are sufficiently necessitated by causes.

We might consider the case of death, for instance. It is generally thought to be necessitated by birth and, thus far, no one who has ever been born has ever not died. We can be reasonably certain — although, again, I want to be wary of an absolute claim here — that death is *necessitated* by birth. Many effects, though, do not seem to be necessitated by their causes in this way. Following Meillassoux, the causal clock model does not abolish the legitimacy of chance, choice, or chaos. Rather, this model merely suggests that *if* an effect is necessitated by its cause, *then* it has already happened in causal time.

2.3 Heat death

If we imagine the extinction of our own species, we will see that it has already occurred on the causal clock. Let's return to our conditions for concurrence:

1. The cause necessitates the effect.
2. The cause has happened.
3. The effect has "sufficient reason."

Does human extinction meet these conditions?

1. The expansion of the universe and the second law of thermodynamics will render the universe unsuitable for life, including human life.
2. The expansion of the universe and the second law of thermodynamics have been set in motion. This may not always be the case but it does seem that we can be reasonably certain that these phenomena are of some order of permanence in our universe. Meillassoux: "Everything could actually collapse: from trees to stars, from stars to laws, from physical laws to logical laws; and this not by virtue of some superior law whereby everything is destined to perish, but by virtue of the absence of any superior law

capable of preserving anything, no matter what, from perishing."[25] Meillassoux argues that a "hyper-Chaos" lies ontologically beneath any physical laws. He may be right, but the expansion of the universe and the second law of thermodynamics need only exist *long enough* to destroy human life, which is not terribly long if one takes a universal view. It is possible, as Meillassoux argues, that an inexistent god could emerge out of the "hyper-Chaos" and create a new universe which is hospitable for life, but it is not obvious that this new life would be equivalent to our species. Humanity *as it has been known* would still be extinct. And, of course, Meillassoux could postulate any entity emerging from his "hyper-Chaos," including a demonic overlord who accelerates human extinction. In regard to the inexistent god, Brassier tells us: "I remain skeptical, since I see no need for any such hypothesis."[26]

3. While hypotheses regarding the cause of human extinction differ to some extent, the causes which necessitate that extinction have almost certainly already been set in motion. One plausible hypothesis predicts the heat death of the universe resulting from the second law of thermodynamics, which William Thomson described as follows:

The result would inevitably be a state of universal rest and death, if the universe were finite and left to obey existing laws. But it is impossible to conceive a limit to the extent of matter in the universe; and therefore science points rather to an endless progress, through an endless space, of action involving the transformation of potential energy into palpable motion and hence into heat, than to a single finite mechanism, running down like a clock, and stopping for ever.[27]

This, of course, assumes that something like global climate

change will not result in human extinction long before entropy tears the universe apart in a violence of accelerating expansion. For our purposes, though, we do not need to be certain of the cause, but only certain *that there is one* — and one that has already been set in motion. If this is the case, and it seems that it is, then we are already extinct in causal time. In *Nihil Unbound*, Brassier puts it this way: "*the solar catastrophe needs to be grasped as something that has already happened*; as the aboriginal trauma driving the history of terrestrial life as an elaborately circuitous detour from stellar death."[28]

It seems that our three conditions are met: human extinction necessarily and sufficiently follows from causes already set in motion. Humanity is thus already extinct in causal time. In fact, it seems that these conditions are met for all species which currently inhabit our planet. Heat death is not speciesist and the expansion of the universe will render the universe alien and inhospitable for all known life. For instance, Brassier, following Lyotard, gives some consideration to the solar catastrophe. Certainly, such a catastrophe would not affect only humans, but would wipe out all life on our planet. It is not just humanity that is already extinct in causal time, but all species on Earth.

2.4 Conflicting temporalities and spatialization

When we go about thinking extinction, we generally employ a colloquial notion of time, abstracted to the appropriate scale. Instead of minutes or days we think of aeons, but the model remains the same. Let's call this model *common-sense time*.

We draw on common-sense time when we say things like "class is at one" or "let's have dinner at six," or when we imagine that effects follow causes and that time is like an arrow. The clock goes forward not back; seconds make up minutes, which make up hours, days, years, decades, and so on.

In common-sense time, extinction is an *event*. It is a thing-that-happens to a species. This conception of extinction is monolithic:

it is a final blow in which the last individual of a species dies, rendering the species historical, distant, past, and often the subject of fantastical imaginings. In this view, there is a "before-extinction," an "extinction-event," and an "after-extinction." The "before-extinction" is a period of normal species-functioning; it contains within it the life and death of every individual (except the last) of a species. It is, essentially, everything we have ever known. The "extinction-event" is the death of the final individual of a species — it is singular, pinpoint-able, and definitive. An "extinction-event" happens *to* a species, e.g., it is what happened to the dinosaurs. The "after-extinction" is the rest of history in which a species is no more. In the after-extinction, life goes on for those species which survived. In this view, extinction has commonalities with death: a period of flourishing proceeds it, it happens to an individual (in this case, a last individual), it is momentary, and life continues after the fact.

This understanding of extinction is neat and linear, it is intuitive — but it is also the product of a misconception about the sort of thing that extinction is. In *Flight Ways*, Thom van Dooren writes: "extinction is never a sharp, singular event...[it is] a slow unraveling of intimately entangled ways of life that begins long before the death of the last individual and continues to ripple forward long afterward..."[29] For van Dooren, extinction is not monolithic but multifaceted, not singular but utterly plural. It is a "slow unraveling" which "begins long before the death of the last individual" contra the notion of a "before-extinction" and "continues to ripple forward long afterward" contra the notion of an "after-extinction." This view ontologically prioritizes process(es); that is, extinction is always a plurality of extinctions. An extinction-event is an event with "rippling" ramifications, not a moment, not the death of a last individual, but a strange mosaic of becoming-nothings.

We can differentiate between extinction in common-sense time and extinction in causal time. Let's call extinction in common-

24

sense time an "extinction-event" and extinction in causal time, "extinctionality." An extinction-event is the fact that states that the death of the last individual of a species has occurred. This is the sort of extinction that is unthinkable for correlationist archaeological theoretic approaches. Extinctionality, on the other hand, is the fact that states that species are always already extinct in causal time. It is the fact of an inevitable extinction which is sufficiently necessitated by events already in motion. There is interplay between an extinction-event and extinctionality: to think extinctionality is to think the inevitability (the already-happenedness) of an extinction-event. This means that extinctionality is also unthinkable for correlationist archaeological theoretic approaches: in order to think extinctionality, thought must think the extinction of thought.

Why should we care about extinction in causal time as opposed to the conceptually intuitive extinction-event of common-sense time? Why is extinctionality a relevant model?

Extinctionality allows us to conceive of extinction as spatialized. In *On an Ungrounded Earth*, Ben Woodard writes: "Time must be spatialized or thought in terms of the becoming-time of space, where space is what remains after temporal succession."[30] If we imagine a cause and effect relationship in which the latter is sufficiently necessitated by the former in causal time, we find that there is no temporal succession; i.e., cause and effect occur concurrently. For Woodard, *space* is what remains after temporal succession. The delta between cause and effect cannot be understood as temporal in causal time because there is no temporal succession. What remains, then, is the "becoming-time of space." Becoming on the causal clock must be understood as spatial.

While an extinction-event relies on temporal succession, extinctionality relies on a spatial succession, i.e., the "becoming-time of space." Woodard again: "Time and space are each the trace of the other leaving behind materiality, a materiality which confirms the mortality of both the living and the non-living..."[31] Where Woodard considers time and space, we should consider an extinction-event (temporal succession) and extinctionality (spatial succession): "an extinction-event and extinctionality are each the trace of the other leaving behind a materiality..." An extinction-event is the trace of extinctionality — it is the actualization of the inevitable, the manifestation of extinctionality. Extinctionality is the trace of an extinction-event — it is the fact of that extinction-event's necessitation by a sufficient cause. For Woodard, the materiality that follows from the time/space interplay "confirms the mortality of both the living and non-living." How can we understand what follows from the extinction-event/extinctionality interplay?

Let's consider the two bifocally, i.e., let's imagine that we can flip back and forth between common-sense and causal time (temporal succession and spatial succession). *What follows?* Extinctionality manifests itself as inevitability in common-sense time, and an extinction-event manifests itself as an actualization of that inevitability in causal time. The common-thread is *inevitability.* For both models of time, extinction is inevitable — it is inextricable from what it means to be a species. This inextricability is like Woodard's "materiality": it confirms the extinctionality of all species.

2.5 Radicalizing Heidegger: species as species-towards-extinction

We can radicalize Heidegger's notion of *Sein-zum-Tode* (Being-towards-death) past the anthropomorphism of Heidegger's Dasein to better understand what this might mean. In *Being and Time,* Heidegger writes:

When, however, one tacitly regards this entity ontologically as something present-at-hand "in time", any attempt at an ontological characterization of the Being "between" birth and death will break down. Dasein does not fill up a track or stretch "of life" — one which is somehow present-at-hand — with the phases of its momentary actualities. It stretches *itself* along in such a way that its own Being is constituted in advance as a stretching-along. The "between" which relates to birth and death already lies *in the Being* of Dasein...Factical Dasein exists as born; and, as born, it is already dying, in the sense of Being-towards-death.[32]

Let's rewrite the final sentence for our own purposes: "*our species exists as born; and, as born, it is already extinct, in the sense of species-towards-extinction.*" In the birth of a species is the extinction in causal time of that same species, in *creation ex nihilo* is always already *annihilation in nihilo*. Species-being as being a species-towards-extinction denotes the inextricability of extinctionality.

Consider this passage from Henri Bergson, in *Matter and Memory*: "I am in the presence of images, in the vaguest sense of the word, images perceived when my senses are opened to them, unperceived when they are closed...as a perfect knowledge of these laws [the laws of nature] would probably allow us to calculate and to foresee what will happen in each of these images, *the future of the images must be contained in their present and will add to them nothing new.*"[33]

Let's replace "images" with "species" in the last bit of that passage: "*The future of the [species] must be contained in their present and will add to them nothing new.*" What is the future of the species that must be contained in their present? In 2.3, we said that all of the species and forms of life currently living on Earth are already extinct in causal time. That is, the future of all species on Earth is extinction — this is the inevitability which is found at the intersection of extinctionality and an extinction-event. That future — extinction — is "contained in their present and will add to them nothing new": our species-extinction is always already inextricable from our species-being. To be a species at all is to be a species-towards-extinction.

In *Radical Atheism*, Martin Hägglund writes: "From within its very constitution life is threatened by death, memory is threatened by forgetting, identity is threatened by alterity, and so on."[34] Death is an interiority for life, forgetting for memory, and alterity for identity. The threat is not external, but always within the "very constitution" of a thing. The greatest threat a species faces, extinction, is not an external threat but an interior one.

For Heidegger, the birth of Dasein contains within it an already-dying — this is "Being-towards-death." This already-dying, this Being-towards-death, is — following Hägglund — interior to the birth of Dasein. A conception of Dasein as anthropocentric or particular to humans undercuts our experience as being qua being, which is an experience of inter-species entanglement. Together, Heidegger and Hägglund show us that species are threatened by extinction not only from exteriorities — from things-that-happen — but also "from within their very constitution" — from their interiorities, from their nature and the nature of things.

This interior extinctionality is not merely a product of organic animation, of being qua being-alive, but of existence *as such*. Consider our terrestrial home for instance, which will one day be obliterated unto dust or gas or bits. In *Cyclonopedia*, Reza Negarestani writes: "...the Tellurian Omega — the utter degradation of the Earth as a Whole. As the ultimate Desert or Xenodrome, the Tellurian Omega engineers a place of utter immanence with the Sun where the communication can no longer be discriminated from what is communicated to the Sun. Xenodrome is the Earth of becoming-Gas or cremation-to-Dust."[35] We have similarly constructed a Xenospecies: the species of becoming-extinct or becoming-nothing, of species *as* species-towards-extinction.

2.6 Schellingian extinction

It might be tempting to flee from the implications of this Heideggerian/Hägglundian radicalization by anthropomorphizing "species-towards-extinction," declaring extinction to be an anthropogenic phenomenon. The Holocene extinction (the sixth mass extinction-event, our current age of extinctions) is often termed the "Anthropocene" extinction. This terminology ontologically prioritizes exteriorities over interiorities, it emphasizes that extinction is human-caused or human-driven rather than interior to species-being as species-towards-extinction.

The ramifications of this prioritization are serious. If the cause which sufficiently necessitates the effect of extinction is humanity, if extinctionality *as such* is anthropogenic, the elimination of humanity would seem to be the *sine qua non* of any morality.

Some extinction-events may be precipitated by anthropogenic factors. The correlation between anthropogenic global climate change and the Holocene extinction is not accidental, but it does not quite imply causation either. Certain extinction-events may happen *when they do* or *in the way that they do* because of anthropogenic circumstances. Extinctionality *as such*, though, is interior to species-being. Again, following Heidegger and Hägglund, extinctionality must be understood as the nature of things. In the same way that death is necessitated by the birth of Dasein, extinction is necessitated by the birth of a species. Annihilation is integral, not incidental.

In *First Outline of a System of the Philosophy of Nature*, F.W.J. Schelling writes: "The product is originally nothing but a mere point, a mere limit, and it is only through Nature's battling against this point that it is, so to speak, raised to a full sphere, a product."[36] Schelling's "Nature" is constantly battling *against* existence — the "mere point" or "mere limit," and this battle is what makes a "product" of Nature fully a product. For Schelling, existence is always existence *against* Nature; extinction is seen as interior to being such that existence appears interruptive.

Schelling illustrates the interruptivity of existence with the analogy of a whirlpool: "The whirlpool is not something immobilized, it is rather something constantly transforming — but reproduced anew at each moment. Thus no product of nature is fixed, but is introduced at each instant through the forces of nature entire."[37]

We can imagine a Schellingian conception of extinction by replacing "product" with "species" — *"the [species] is originally nothing but a mere point, a mere limit, and it is only through Nature's battling against this point that it is, so to speak, raised to a full sphere, a [species]."* The existence of a species is an existence *against* nature — this is what it means to be a species, to exist interruptively. A species-towards-extinction is a species-against-nature because extinction is "onto-genic," which is to say that it is generated by existence, that it is interior to existence in the sense of species-towards-extinction. Only particular extinction-events are anthropogenic and, even in these cases, anthropogenesis is an acceleration of onto-genesis rather than a cause in-itself.

3

Extinction and Materials

3.1 The differentiation of species

How do we differentiate between species? A discussion of the distinctness of species — of how thick or thin the line between species is — will have to be relegated to another project but, for us, it is enough simply to say that species are in some sense distinct from one another.

In *On the Origin of Species*, Darwin writes of the definition of a "species": "No one definition has satisfied all naturalists; yet every naturalist knows vaguely what he means when he speaks of a species. Generally, the term includes the unknown element of a distinct act of creation."[38] Even in Darwin's day, there was little agreement on what made a species distinct. It was clear that species were distinct — for instance, that a salmon was not a monkey — but it was unclear what the characteristic difference was. This remains the case in contemporary discourse.

What is the characteristic difference between a salmon and a monkey? It might be claimed that the difference is phenomenal, that a salmon and a monkey have distinctive subjectivities. Perhaps all species are distinct inasmuch as their phenomenalities are distinct. The problem is that we have no way to contrast these phenomenalities without a reduction to embodiment.

We imagine that a salmon has a phenomenal experience distinct from a monkey because a salmon has a different form or shape than a monkey; it looks different or is differently embodied. Even if phenomenality is the distinctive feature of a species, our vantage point cannot prove epistemically fruitful. In his pivotal essay "What Is It Like to Be a Bat," Thomas Nagel considers the phenomenal experience of a bat: "Reflection on what it is like to be a bat seems to lead us, therefore to the conclusion that there are facts that do not consist in the truth of propositions expressible in a human language. We can be compelled to recognize the existence of such facts without being able to state or comprehend them."[39]

That is, what it is *like* to be a bat (or a salmon, monkey, etc.) is a fact that does not "consist in the truth of propositions expressible in the human language." We may be compelled to admit that it is like something to be a bat or salmon or monkey, but we are unable "to state or comprehend" what it might be like.

Since we cannot state or comprehend what it is like to be a monkey or a salmon, we cannot differentiate between what it is like to be those species. We cannot contrast what we cannot know. It follows that we cannot differentiate between their phenomenalities. The comparisons that we draw must be material — to be a distinct species is to be distinctly manifested in material.

3.2 A dichotomous choice?

Let's consider an obvious objection: the argument in 3.1 presents a false dichotomy. The differentiation between species is not either a difference in phenomenality or a difference in material manifestation. This dichotomous choice leaves out differences in lineage or behavior, among other possible differentiations.

This objection is the result of a misunderstanding: the objector imagines that we are asking about the *actual* distinctness of species, rather than the way in which we *know* that species are distinct. Our question is epistemological rather than ontological. As we discussed in 3.1, it may very well be the case that species are *actually* distinct phenomenally. That being said, we cannot *know* their distinctiveness except materially.

How do we know that the lineage of one species is different from another? How do we know that they act differently or have different habits? In each of these cases, the difference is materially manifested. A difference in lineage is discovered via the fossil record or via other species with similar embodiments — these things are empirically observable because they are *things*, they are material. A difference in behavior is discovered because it is observed. Differences in behavior might include eating habits or defenses against predators. The distinctiveness of an eating habit is embodied — a species eats distinctively insofar as its eating is distinctively embodied and its food, too, is distinctively embodied. The distinctiveness of a defense against predators is also embodied — a species defends itself distinctively insofar as it uses its embodiment distinctively for the purpose of defense.

In both cases — those of lineage and behavior — the difference is manifested materially. We *discover* fossils which illustrate lineage or we *see* behavior; these are observations of material things and the differences that we find are material differences. In light of this, let us consider the case of Australopithecus anew. *Is Australopithecus distinct insofar as it is distinct materially?*

Here, the objector might issue a rejoinder: our reductive account fails to explain three distinct elements of species-being: phenomenality, ideology, and artifactual culture. Phenomenality may be behind an epistemic wall, but it may still be distinctive. If other species can have ideologies, surely these are distinctive (the cultural-historical archaeologist would argue this regarding human cultures as well). And, species distinctively impact their environments, making and using things in a way that is not reducible to material embodiment.

In response to this rejoinder, let's proceed by *reductio*:

1. Phenomenality — even if phenomenality differs across species with no relation to species' embodiment, we cannot know or think this difference. The objector assumes that there can be distinction beyond an epistemic wall. Distinction in-itself, though, is an epistemic praxis:

one contrasts or searches for difference in the pursuit of knowledge, nature itself cannot contrast. Nature may make species distinct, but it cannot ruminate on this difference. The notion that distinction can lie beyond Nagel's epistemic wall is thus a contradiction in terms: distinction *is* epistemic.

2. Ideology — there is, at the very least, one species capable of possessing an ideology: humans. We might also concede, contra anthropocentrism, that species such as Australopithecus could have been capable of complex thought processes which resulted in a thought-systemization similar in scope and impact to human ideologies. This is probably not the case for *all* species. Consider a snail and a rabbit: the two are distinct and yet it would seem strange, albeit possible, to suggest that either a snail or a rabbit have distinctive ideologies. If ideologies are the chief distinctive characteristic, the vast majority of species begin to blur into one another.

3. Artifactual Culture — the objector tells us that all species make and use material things or alter their environments in material ways. These material manifestations or residues across species are "artifactual cultures." "Artifact," here, is meant in the broad sense of the material residue of species-being, of the existence of a species. Artifacts escape our account of the reduction of species to species' embodiment. They are an integral part of species-being; the way in which they are made or used is intertwined with species' embodiment and is thus inextricable from being a particular species.

We can dismiss (1) and (2) and take (3) into account: our reduction must be expanded to include both embodiment and artifactual culture. To be a distinctive species is both to be distinctively embodied and to have distinctive "artifacts," — again, in the broad sense of making and using material things or altering the environment in material ways.

3.3 A relation of subsumption

Recall, from 2.4, the way in which we differentiated between extinction in common-sense time and extinction in causal time. We termed the former an "extinction-event" and the latter, "extinctionality." An extinction-event is the fact of the death of the last individual of a species and extinctionality is the fact of species-being as inextricable from being a species-towards-extinction, i.e., a species is always already extinct in causal time.

In light of this, we can construct two premises:

> From 2.5: A species is always already extinct in causal time, i.e., species-being is inextricable from extinctionality (i.e., being a species-towards-extinction).
> From 3.2: Species-being is manifested materially, viz., in embodiment and artifactual culture.

Let's use these premises syllogistically:

1. Extinctionality (A) is inextricable from species-being (B).
2. Species-being (B) is manifested materially (C).
3. Extinctionality (A) is manifested materially (C).

(3) entails a relation of subsumption between materiality and extinctionality: materiality is subsumed under extinctionality such that extinctionality is manifested in the materiality of a species.

What is meant by "subsumption"? In the *Critique of Pure Reason*, Kant understands the relation between the categories of understanding and the manifold to be one of subsumption. This is the reification of the correlation: the mental structures the real, manifesting itself in the real in such a way that the real is structured by the mental and nothing besides.

Kant writes: "to the use of a concept there also belongs a function of the power of judgement, whereby an object is subsumed under it..."[40] For Kant, the particular is brought into a relation with the universal via a relation of subsumption, i.e., via a method of abstraction in which the truth of the universal is made manifest in the particular.

Consider (3) above: in the same way that — for Kant — the mental manifests itself in the real such that the real is structured by the mental, extinctionality manifests itself in the material such that the material is structured by extinctionality.

In 1.4, we employed Heidegger's threefold conditions of death to think about human extinction. The first condition was one's "ownmost potentiality-for-being."[41] This means that death is the thing that makes Dasein distinctive. Applied to extinction, we interpreted the "ownmost potentiality-for-being" as the notion that extinction (how, when, why, etc.) is the thing that makes a species distinctive.

In 2.5, we employed Heidegger's "Being-towards-death" to think about extinction, radicalizing it to become species-towards-extinction. This means that extinctionality is inextricable from species-being.

In 3.2, we reduced species-being to a species' material manifestation (embodiment and artifactual culture).

(3), therefore, follows from 1.4, 2.5, and 3.2: the thing that makes a species distinctive is its extinctionality, that extinctionality is inextricable from species-being, and that species-being is manifested materially. Extinctionality is made manifest in species-being, which is made manifest in material. Our syllogism, again:

1. Extinctionality (A) is made manifest in/is inextricable from species-being (B).

2. Species-being (B) is manifested in material, i.e., embodiment and artifactual culture (C).
3. Extinctionality (A) is made manifest in material (C).

(3) is simply the conclusion that follows from 1.4, 2.5, and 3.2: the relation of subsumption is such that extinctionality is manifested in materiality; materiality is structured by extinctionality and nothing besides. The essence of the material thing is subsumed under the facticity of extinction. This is true, of course, both for human materiality and for Australopithecus' materiality. The extinctionality of Australopithecus is manifested in the artifacts discovered at Lomekwi 3; the artifacts are the residue of Australopithecus' annihilation.

4

The Phenomenal/Real Collapse

4.1 Escaping the resurrection

Let's briefly recapitulate: in 1.2, we considered three correlationist archaeological theoretic approaches: post-processual archaeology, cultural-historical archaeology, and post-modernist archaeology. We then problematized these approaches in regard to the question of what it would be like to be an Australopithecus who made or used the artifacts discovered at Lomekwi 3. We found that these archaeological theoretic approaches perform a resurrection of Australopithecus as human in such a way that Australopithecus becomes extinct-for-us, rather than extinct *as such*.

In 2.1, we defined "causal time," in which a cause and an effect that is sufficiently necessitated by that cause occur concurrently. Then, in 2.3 and 2.4, we considered a way in which we might already be extinct and reconceptualized species as species-towards-extinction (Heidegger) and extinctionality as an interiority, within the "very constitution" of a species (Hägglund).

In 3.3, we explored the relation of subsumption between materiality and extinctionality. The extinctionality of Australopithecus was shown to be manifested in the artifacts at Lomekwi 3 such that the artifacts are structured by that extinctionality and nothing besides.

In each of these sections, we encountered similar problems which drive the anthropomorphism of the archaeological theoretic approaches — these are problems of phenomenality. In 1.2, we examined Meillassoux's critique of "correlationism": we saw that post-processual, cultural-historical, and post-modernist archaeological theoretic approaches correlate being with thought such that neither can be understood to exist independently. We can restate the correlation of being and thought as the correlation of the real and the phenomenal. The real and the phenomenal are distinct but dependent on one another. In 2.1, our phenomenal experience of time, which we termed "common-sense" time, was shown to be inadequate on its own for thinking extinction. In 3.2, we encountered an objection regarding our reduction of species-being to materiality: the reduction fails to account for phenomenality. Each of these issues relies on a mutual dependence and distinction between the real and the phenomenal. This version of Meillassoux's correlation stands in the way of our task — to escape the resurrection of Australopithecus as human. If we are going to escape the resurrection, we have to allow the real to be uncorrelated with the phenomenal. That is, we have to escape our "selves."

4.2 Metzinger's "nemocentrism"

In *Being No One*, Thomas Metzinger advocates a "nemocentric" approach to the real-phenomenal distinction. He describes this approach as follows:

> Its main thesis is that no such things as selves exist in the world: Nobody ever was or had a self. All that ever existed were conscious self-models that could not be recognized as models. The phenomenal self is not a thing, but a process — and the subjective experience of being someone emerges if a conscious information-processing system operates under a transparent self-model. You are such a system right now, as you read these sentences. Because you cannot recognize your self-model as a model, it is transparent: you look right through it. You don't see it. But you see with it.[42]

Metzinger seeks to explain the phenomenal via a reduction to a transparent "self-model." This is a representational explanation:

39

the phenomenal is explained as an internal "map of the world" which possesses a "certain isomorphy" to external reality.[43] For Metzinger, the "self-model" of a phenomenality is the "computational tool" of a complex carbon-based information-processing system that aids the organism in "owning its own hardware."[44]

"The phenomenal self is not a thing, but a process..." — this is the process of self-modeling that an organism uses in order to engage with external reality: *"You don't see it. But you see with it."*

For Metzinger, phenomenality "is not a substance or an individual — be it physical or nonphysical — but an ongoing process: the process of self-modeling, as currently integrated into working memory and the organism's globally available world-model."[45]

It might be objected that Metzinger's nemocentrism involves a conception of the phenomenal as illusory or unreal. If the objector is right, nemocentrism is no better than new-age mysticisms that proclaim that "enlightenment" is reached by letting go of the illusion of being someone. These new-age mysticisms are, of course, deeply influenced by Eastern traditions. Consider Dōgen: "Just practice good, do good for others, without thinking of making yourself known so that you may gain reward. Really bring benefit to others, gaining nothing for yourself. This is the primary requisite for *breaking free of attachments to the Self.*"[46]

Metzinger wants to explain the phenomenal, rather than explain it away. The phenomenal self is not illusory, but can be explained representationally. It is the transparent "process of self-modeling" that an organism undergoes. Metzinger is not advocating that we follow Dōgen, becoming experiencing non-subjects. Instead, we become experience-less subjects: we see our "selves" to be no-one and no-where.[47] Metzinger shows phenomenal selves to be material processes, reducible to material, albeit a sort of material that can undergo the complex processes which we term "having a phenomenal self."

4.3 The phenomenal/real distinction

A nemocentric approach allows us to collapse the distinction and mutual dependence between phenomenal experience and external reality, or "the real." Phenomenal experience is the "thought" of the thought/being correlation, it is the inescapable human mode of correlationist archaeological theoretic approaches. The real is that which is not contextualized, not correlated to thought, and outside of human modes. This is what Meillassoux calls the "great outdoors" (Meillassoux 2006: 7). Again: "the *absolute* outside of pre-critical thinkers: that outside which was not relative to us..."[48]

For Metzinger, the correlation between the real and the phenomenal can be collapsed. The phenomenal just is a representation of the real, of the "great outdoors" or the "absolute outside." This does not lead to a Cartesian or Berkeleyan solipsism, nor to Dōgen's "breaking free of attachments to the Self," but rather to a materialism in which correlationist archaeological theoretic approaches are revealed as making a fundamental mistake: they presuppose that "selves" exist. Metzinger reveals this mistake: "All that exists are certain information-processing systems meeting the constraints for phenomenality while operating under a transparent self-model. At least for all conscious beings so far known to us, it is true that they neither have nor are a self."[49]

Foucault famously wrote that "man is an invention of recent date. And one perhaps nearing its end."[50] For Metzinger, man (as a phenomenal self) is an invention of ancient date — it is likely that the phenomenal representation of external reality has a long and illustrious history — but also "one perhaps nearing its end." At least, insofar as man is thought to be distinct from and dependent on the real. Metzinger sees the phenomenal "self-model" as a virtuality produced by a carbon-based information-processing system, showing Foucault's "end" to be a collapse. The invention of phenomenal man is just that, an invention. This is not to delegitimize the invention, but to see it as a simulacrum of sorts, and thus to collapse the distinctiveness and mutual dependence of the correlation.

4.4 Disintegrating Sellars' "manifest image of man-in-the-world"

In "Philosophy and the Scientific Image of Man," Wilfrid Sellars differentiates between the "manifest image of man-in-the-world" and the "scientific image." The manifest image is an image of intentions and appearances. It is the "thought" of the correlation, the contextualization, culturalization, linguistification, and humanization of being. It may be refined via comparison to external reality ("correlational induction") but is tied to that which is thinkable or perceptible.

The scientific image, on the other hand, is an image of man-in-the-world as seen by theoretical sciences. It sees man as made up of particles and restrained by physical forces and it theorizes about causality.

For Sellars, these two images can both be complementary at times and in conflict at other times. Take, for instance, the following quotation from Hume:

> In every system of morality, which I have hitherto met with, I have always remarked, that the author proceeds for some time in the ordinary way of reasoning, and establishes the being of a God, or makes observations concerning human affairs; when of a sudden I am surprised to find, that instead of the usual copulations of propositions, is, and is not, I meet with no proposition that is not connected with an *ought*, or an *ought not*. This change is imperceptible; but is, however, of the last consequence. For as this *ought*, or *ought not*, expresses some new relation or affirmation, 'tis necessary that it should be observed and explained; and at the same time that a reason should be given, for what seems altogether inconceivable,

how this new relation can be a deduction from others, which are entirely different from it.[51]

For Hume, the conflation between an "is" and an "ought" is troubling. This can be understood, following Sellars, as a conflation between the scientific image and the manifest image. The scientific image describes the world, particularly employing locutions informed by theoretical sciences. The manifest image is often prescriptive, making normative statements about how the world ought to be, particularly employing locutions informed by religion, moral philosophy, and the like. In this sense, the two images are often in conflict.

Here's another example, this time from Brassier: theoretical physics tells us that objects which are perceived as solid are often largely composed of empty space. The scientific image sees the empty space, the manifest image sees the solid object. Sellars prioritizes the scientific image over the manifest image but allows for their coexistence in an overall synoptic vision.[52]

Of the manifest image, Sellars writes: "For it is no merely incidental feature of man that he has a conception of himself as man-in-the-world, just as it is obvious, on reflection, that 'if man had a radically different conception of himself he would be a radically different kind of man.'"[53]

In Meillassoux's correlation, the two images are complementary: it is claimed that one cannot be understood without the other. For us, this is problematic, because thinking extinction entails the collapse of this correlation. *How can this be achieved?*

"If man had a radically different conception of himself he would be a radically different kind of man" — in light of this, consider Metzinger's nemocentrism. A "radically different kind of man" is exactly what must be generated to escape the correlation; the manifest image must be collapsed into the scientific image.

Of the scientific image, Sellars writes: "It is in the scientific image of man-in-the-world that we begin to see the main outlines of the way in which man came to have an image of himself-in-the-world."[54] This is Metzinger's representational explanation: man "came to have an image of himself-in-the-world" because the phenomenal man is a "self-model" of the external reality of the world. A nemocentric approach explains the manifest image as a virtuality of the scientific image, collapsing the distinction and thus the correlation.

Brassier diagnoses Meillassoux's correlationism as a tendency among continental philosophies which share a "more or less profound hostility to the idea that the scientific image describes 'what there really is,' that it has an ontological purchase capable of undermining man's manifest self-conception as a person or intentional agent."[55] Archaeological theoretic approaches, like continental philosophies, share this tendency towards a "more or less profound hostility to the idea that the scientific image describes" what is and towards the idea that the scientific image has "an ontological purchase capable of undermining man's manifest self-conception." Metzinger's nemocentrism does that undermining, granting ontological purchase to the scientific image and collapsing the phenomenal into the real.

Analogy and Assemblages

5.1 Artifacts and embodiments

Let's situate ourselves by recounting in brief some of our previous arguments. In 2.3 and 2.4, we argued that a species is always already extinct in causal time, i.e., to be a species is to be a species-towards-extinction. A human archaeologist, then, is always already extinct in causal time, extinctionality being within the "very constitution" — interior to — the archaeologist.

In 3.2, we reduced the distinctiveness of species-being to a material distinctiveness. Then, in 3.3, we argued that extinctionality is manifested in materiality such that materiality is structured by extinctionality and nothing besides.

In 4.2, we reduced the phenomenal to a representational construct of the material (a carbon-based information-processing system). The phenomenality of a species, which so preoccupied us in 3.2, can thus be reduced to a representational construct of a material assemblage (an assemblage of carbon-based information-processing systems). An "assemblage" denotes a constellation of things, and an "assemblage-materiality" denotes the constellation of material things to which species-being is reducible.

Recall from 3.2 that the materials of a species are either embodied materials or artifacts, the former understood as the material embodiment of a species (including the carbon-based information-processing component) and the latter understood as the material which a species makes or uses, or the material way in which a species impacts its environment. Let's term the former an "embodiment-materiality" and the latter an "artifact-materiality." Together, embodiment-materiality and artifact-materiality make up the materiality of a species, i.e., a species' assemblage-materiality.

How can an extinction-event be understood in relation to the assemblage-materiality of a species? An extinction-event is the partial dissolution of the assemblage-materiality of a species; it leaves a species' artifact-materiality intact but annihilates a species' embodiment-materiality. What happened during Australopithecus' extinction-event (extinction in common-sense time, the death of the last Australopithecus individual)?

Australopithecus' artifact-materiality remained (and elements of this were discovered at Lomekwi 3), while Australopithecus' embodiment-materiality was annihilated, i.e., there are no more embodied Australopithecus individuals.

5.2 Deleuzo-Guattarian territorializations

In *A Thousand Plateaus*, Deleuze and Guattari respond to Hume's problem of personal identity. Hume considers the question of how I know that I am still the same person who was born however many years ago to my mother. For Hume, personal identity is simply the product of habit; we are habitually habitual and one of our many habits is to expect the future to be like the past. I know that the sun is going to rise tomorrow because *it always has*; similarly, I know that I am the same person because *I always have been*.

In response to this, Deleuze and Guattari define the self as an assemblage of objects, each partial. In this sense, the self is conceived of as city-like. These partial objects are assembled together to constitute an identity. "Territorialization" is this act of constitution: parts are organized into a cohesive or semi-cohesive whole that can be called a "territory." "Territory" can be thought of as essentially city-like, i.e., the assemblage has some sort of unity but both the whole (the city) and the parts remain — in some sense — independent or on separate and distinct planes of understanding.

The birth or creation of a species can be understood as a

Deleuzo-Guattarian "territorialization." A multiplicity of objects are brought into relation (embodiments and artifacts) which constitute the species-being of a particular species. The coming-into-being of a species is the occurrence of a territorialization: a territory of species-being is constituted which consists in the sum total of the artifact-materiality and embodiment-materiality of a species. We previously defined this as the "assemblage-materiality" of a species. This assemblage-materiality is the territory of species-being.

Territorialization can be understood as the attachment of a sign to its context of signification: the coming-into-being of a species can be understood as the attachment of artifact-materiality to embodiment-materiality. Artifact-materiality is the sign of species-being (consider Lomekwi 3) and embodiment-materiality is the context of signification (rendering the artifacts discovered at Lomekwi 3 intelligible). In order to understand the artifacts, we have to understand how Australopithecus made or used them: this is the context of signification.

We previously described an extinction-event as the partial dissolution of an assemblage-materiality, i.e., the partial dissolution of the territory of a particular species' species-being. An extinction-event can thus be understood as a "deterritorialization." It is the detachment of a sign from its context of signification via the obliteration of the context of signification. A territory (assemblage-materiality) is deterritorialized, leaving only artifact-materiality. This presents a problem for the archaeologist: the artifact-materiality of a species cannot be properly understood without an understanding of the embodiment-materiality of a species. Extinction obliterates the context of signification by subtracting the species which provides or grants that context. The sign (an artifact) is thus rendered unintelligible.

The deterritorialization of an extinction-event is partial; it leaves behind a territory constituted only by artifact-materiality.

Archaeology, then, must be understood as a "reterritorialization." Reterritorialization can be understood as the (usually partial) reconstitution of the sign-context relationship (often via the construction of a new context of signification). The scientific project does not stop at deterritorialization but proceeds to construct a new, scientific context of signification that can serve to better render the sign intelligible. The archaeologist cannot reconstitute the territory of Australopithecus' assemblage-materiality, so another way must be found to understand Australopithecus' artifact-materiality. The sign must be granted a new context of signification.

What is this new context of signification? How can artifact-materiality be understood when deterritorialized from embodiment-materiality?

5.3 Epistemic ground, the earthwormic dialectic, and material analogy

In 3.3, we defined the relationship between materiality and extinctionality as one of subsumption. Materiality is subsumed under extinctionality such that extinctionality manifests itself in materiality. Australopithecus' artifact-materiality, insofar as it is material, can thus be understood as a manifestation of extinctionality.

The nemocentric archaeologist, who understands phenomenal experience to be a material virtuality and the manifest image to be a representational construct of the scientific image, has essentially materialized himself. The nemocentric archaeologist can also be understood as a manifestation of extinctionality.

The reterritorialization of archaeology can proceed by analogy: both artifact-materiality and the nemocentric archaeologist are manifestations of extinctionality. This commonality allows the archaeologist to analogize. Let's term this analogical process "material analogy." Does material analogy have any epistemic ground?

Material analogy reconstitutes the territory of species-being by replacing the embodiment-materiality of Australopithecus with the nemocentric embodiment-materiality of the archaeologist. The archaeologist, stripped of the phenomenal/real distinction, can analogize between human experience and Australopithecus' experience. This allows us to make legitimate scientific claims about what it would be like to be the Australopithecus who made or used the artifacts discovered at Lomekwi 3 — this is what it means to understand Lomekwi 3 through the lens of Sellar's scientific image.

It's important to note that material analogy is speculative. To analogize is to speculate about likeness: material analogy engages in a speculative reterritorialization. It will be helpful to consider Reza Negarestani's "Drafting the Inhuman: Conjectures on Capitalism and Organic Necrocracy" here. He notes: "With the burgeoning popularity of speculative thought, it is becoming more evident that what is labelled as 'speculative' is more an epiphenomenon of the inquisitive renegotiation of human faculties, their limits and vulnerabilities, rather than a counterintuitive foray into the abyssal vistas unlocked by contemporary science."[56] The method of material analogy attempts the latter rather than the former. The renegotiation of human faculties (and the limits and vulnerabilities of those faculties) too often simply reifies the correlation, undermining the work that was set out to be achieved. Material analogy thus says nothing of human faculties or capacities — other than the simple building of analogical relations — but rather is a "foray into the abyssal vistas unlocked by contemporary science." Correlationism renders deterritorialization *absolute*: for the correlationist, there is no hope for the reconstitution of assemblage-materiality because the analogical process undertaken is interrupted at every turn by the inescapability of modes or contexts. It cannot think the "abyssal vistas" of contemporary science because those vistas *do not exist* for it.

The method of material analogy is a method of making real those vistas: of acknowledging the abyss of deterritorialization and still (Negarestani's "counterintuitive foray") attempting to reterritorialize/reconstitute assemblage-materiality via analogy.

Territorialization, deterritorialization, and reterritorialization can be understood as dialectical and the archaeologist qua reterritorializer or reconsituter of territory qua species-being can be understood as the synthetic actor. The archaeologist takes on the role of the earthworm. The coming-into-being of organic life is a sort of territorialization; it constitutes a particular territory of animated matter; it is the "thesis" of our dialectical analogy. The decay or annihilative putrefaction of death and post-death is a sort of deterritorialization; it de-constitutes a particular territory of animated matter; it is the "antithesis" of our dialectic. The earthwormic praxis (material analogy) is a sort of reterritorialization; the earthworm is fueled by decay — it is saprophytic — and this essentially reconstitutes the original territory, albeit incompletely. Archaeology can be similarly understood as earthwormic or saprophytic: fueled by the decay of embodiment-materiality. The fact that this decay is not absolute but partial, the fact that artifact-materiality survives an extinction-event, makes archaeology as such possible.

The epistemic ground for this method is found in this overarching territorial ontology, which we will term the "earthwormic dialectic." Material analogy is possible because artifact-materiality survives an extinction-event. The deterritorialization of an extinction-event is not total but partial; there is still territory — namely, artifact-materiality — after an extinction-event; *ipso facto*, archaeological analysis is made possible.

Material analogy is a Levinasian face to face encounter with the extinctionality of the Other. This analogical reterritorialized relationship is asymmetrical: the extinctionality of the Other is prioritized vis-à-vis the extinctionality of the self. Material analogy is thus a self-abnegation, an opening-up, which grounds archaeology. This self-abnegation results from the face to face encounter with the extinctionality of the Other (see 6.3.4 for an elaboration of the face to face encounter with the extinctionality of the Other).

One lingering problem remains if we are to render the artifacts discovered at Lomekwi 3 intelligible. The commonality that we found between our nemocentric materiality and the artifact-materiality of Australopithecus is that both are manifestations of extinctionality. It remains the case, though, that thinking extinction requires thinking the extinction of thought, and our current ontologies, mired in correlationism, do not allow for this.

6

Thinking Annihilation

6.1 Thinking the extinction of thought

In 5.3, we detailed a specific territorial ontology, following Deleuze and Guattari, that we termed the "earthwormic dialectic." This ontology legitimized material analogy, allowing a nemocentric archaeologist to analogize between human embodiment-materiality and the artifact-materiality of Australopithecus by reterritorializing Australopithecus' assemblage-materiality.

This ontology can think the artifacts discovered at Lomekwi 3; it allows us to make a statement in this form: "*Australopithecus made or used the artifacts discovered at Lomekwi 3.*" The earthwormic dialectic — and, more specifically, material analogy — renders the artifacts discovered at Lomekwi 3 intelligible. What about a statement in this form: "*Australopithecus made or used the artifacts discovered at Lomekwi 3 prior to its extinction*"?

Recall from 1.3 and 1.4 the resurrection of Australopithecus as human (the quasi-Australopithecus), which the question of *what it would be like to be the Australopithecus who made or used the artifacts discovered at Lomekwi 3* brought about. In 1.4, we were left with the following scientific claim: "*the Australopithecus-for-us who made or used these artifacts-for-us is extinct-for-us.*"

The earthwormic dialectic allows us to rewrite this sentence as: "*the Australopithecus who made or used these artifacts is extinct-for-us.*" The dialectic renders intelligible that which fits within its territorial ontology; Australopithecus-for-us becomes Australopithecus' embodiment-materiality and the artifacts-for-us become Australopithecus' artifact-materiality. Together, this constitutes Australopithecus' assemblage-materiality. In this way, we can understand what happens in an extinction-event, viz., a deterritorialization of Australopithecus' assemblage-materiality. Australopithecus, though, remains extinct-for-us. There are two reasons for this:

1. The method of material analogy requires us to analogize between our own materiality (understood nemocentrically) and the artifact-materiality of Australopithecus. This is framed as an analogization between our extinctionality and Australopithecus' extinctionality. Thinking Australopithecus' extinctionality requires us to think our own extinctionality.
2. Thinking our own extinctionality means thinking the extinction of thought. The earthwormic dialectic does not explain how thought can think its own extinction.

Insofar as (2) is the case, a being/thought correlation remains intact within archaeological theoretic approaches in regard to extinction. Our task will be to eradicate this correlation, allowing thought to think the extinction of thought. To this end, let's briefly review the correlation:

The history of Kantian and post-Kantian philosophy has been the history of a singular notion: there can be no existence without existents. That is, existence *as such* cannot exist uninstantiated; existence is always existence-of. This notion takes three distinct forms: the Kantian form, the form of the correlational circle, and the form of idealism. Kant, in his *Critique of Pure Reason*, understands the relation between the manifest (the real, existence) and the categories of understanding (thought, existents) to be one of subsumption. That is, the thing in-itself exists (although we can be unsure whether there is more than one thing in-itself), but we cannot know it. We can call this the *thesis of human finitude*: there exists an in-itself that is subsumed under our categories of understanding such that we cannot understand it in separation from those categories; it becomes an in-itself for us, rather than an in-itself as such. In this way, Kant privileges the human/

world relation over other relations; we cannot understand the relation — to borrow an example from Islamic philosophy — between cotton and the fire that burns it without always already understanding it *for us*. That is, the relation between fire and cotton, insofar as it can be understood, must always be a relation between fire and cotton and the categories of understanding (thought, a particular existent, etc.). We can call this the *thesis of access*: all world/world relations must be understood as human/world relations.

The form of the correlational circle radicalizes this view: to think the in-itself is always to *think* the in-itself and thus to think a thought. The in-itself is always within thought; to think it is already to have rendered it within the "correlational circle," the circle in which being (the in-itself) is always correlated with, tied to, and unintelligible apart from thought. The thesis of human finitude evolves into the thesis of human incapability: one cannot even say that, following Kant, there exists a thing in-itself that cannot be known. Rather, one must say that the thing in-itself is essentially meaningless. Access to the real, to existence, or being, also evolves: for Kant, all world/world relations must be understood as human/world relations. For the correlational circle, there is uncertainty and ambiguity about whether or not there *are* world/world relations at all. The form of the idealist further radicalizes this view: there can be no in-itself; there is only thought. That is, there can be no existence at all, but only existents; existents exist (although the idealist must find a way not to succumb to solipsism — that is, I know only that one existent (myself) exists), but existence as such does not exist. Human finitude becomes total for the idealist and access becomes impossible.

Each of these distinct forms is a variation of the *thesis of existentiality*: the in-itself (being, existence) must always be correlated with and inseparable from the for-us (thought, existents). There can be no existence without existents. For the

Kantian, existence is "out-there," but cannot be known. The outside, in being understood, is always already an inside; i.e., the manifest is subsumed under the categories of understanding. For the correlationist circle, the phrase "existence is out-there" is meaningless; there might be an in-itself but to think it is already to place it within thought and thus to extinguish its veracity, its possibility. Not only can there be no existence sans existents, there can be no existence outside of existents; existence is always within existents. For the idealist, existence does not exist. There is no outside, but only ever an inside; i.e., not only can there be no existence sans existents, there can be no existence at all. There are only existents, or perhaps only a single existent.

The theoretic models which underlie archaeology each restate the thesis of existentiality. These "existential" archaeologies (existential insofar as they restate the thesis of existentiality), which correlate existence to existents such that the two cannot be understood separately, are philosophies of the Same. For these philosophies, the intelligibility of the Other presupposes the similitude of the Other. That is, the Other is made to be the Same via the correlation between being and thought, existence and existents. The Other outside of context, thought, or the categories of understanding is incomprehensible; even to suggest the existence of this Other is to utter an incoherence. The Other exists only insofar as it exists *for me* and, thus, the Other's existence relies on being made to be the Same, on being an existent. The statement that characterizes much of the history of philosophy is this: to be is to be contained within my categories, to be is to be constrained, to be taxonomically.

The task of this chapter, then, will be to gain access to the outside anew. That is, to find a way in which these philosophies can be reformulated such that existence can be understood sans existents, such that the Other can be posited as the Other qua Other, the Other of radical alterity, rather than the Other qua Same. To that end the philosophy of Levinas will be darkened in order to sketch an alternative: an encounter with the Other qua Other, a non-existential (even, anti-existential) theoretic basis upon which archaeology can *de novo* stand.

6.2 Becoming and extinction

What exactly are we doing when we imagine extinction in causal time *and* common-sense time? In common-sense time, extinction is perceived as a monolithic event in which the last individual of a species dies. In causal time, extinction is perceived of as always already the case.

In 2.4, we tried to imagine common-sense time and causal time bifocally. We found that the common-thread is an inevitability: in both models of time, extinction is inevitable, i.e., extinctionality is inextricable from what it means to be a species. In this sense, bifocal extinction is *becoming*. Perceiving extinction as a becoming, a process of becoming-extinct, just is what it means for extinction to be inevitable. It's going to happen, it *has* happened in one sense, but not quite in another. Causal time sees inevitability without the decay, common-sense time sees decay without the inevitability: together, bifocal time sees extinction as an inevitable decay.

In *Flight Ways*, Thom van Dooren writes: "species are engaged in an ongoing intergenerational process of *becoming* — of adaptation and transformation — in which individual organisms are not so much 'members' of a class or a kind, but 'participants' in an ongoing and evolving way of life."[57] For van Dooren, the becoming of species is a becoming-adapted or becoming-transformed. Extinction, then, is problematic because it interrupts this becoming, disentangling "entangled" ways of life and preventing the normal processes of species from continuing.

Our bifocal sense of time shares van Dooren's proclivity for process, it too entails a becoming, but our becoming of species is a becoming-extinct. If extinction is inevitable decay, it is not an interruption of species' existence (becoming-adapted, etc.). Rather, species' existence is an interruption of annihilation (becoming-extinct).

This ontology, which views forces of decay as archetypal and forces of assembly as interruptive, which reframes Deleuzian monism (becoming) as a pitch-black dynamism (unbecoming, becoming-extinct), will be termed "speculative annihilationism." The word "annihilation" finds its roots in the Latin "ad" (towards) and "nihil" (nothing). Annihilation is being-towards-nothing or becoming-nothing verbatim.

The objectives of the remainder of Chapter 6 will be threefold:

1. Ask: "What does speculative annihilationism involve?"
2. Ask: "How can this ontology allow thought to think the extinction of thought?"
3. Ask: "When thought thinks the extinction of thought, what does it think?"

6.3 What does speculative annihilationism involve?

We have defined speculative annihilationism as a process ontology (i.e., a monistic ontology of becoming) which sees decay as paradigmatic and existence or assemblage as abnormal and exceptional. Let's consider six characteristics of our speculative annihilationism (SA), discussing each in turn:

1. SA is a vitalism.

SA is a dark perversion of vitalism. In *Flight Ways*, van Dooren describes his vitalism as expressed in the fact that "a species is always becoming different from, other than, itself," which he terms "the emergent becoming of a species."[58] For van Dooren, there is an implicit vital force at work — this is a becoming-adapted or transformed, the becoming-entangled of various forms of life. Extinction prevents this becoming and is

SA is a vitalism

thus interruptive.

SA's "vital" force is — contra van Dooren — not one of life, generativity, or adaptivity, but is rather a collection of various forces (see characteristic 2) which are disintegrating, degenerative, disadaptive, and decaying. SA is a vitalism insofar as it is an ontology of process, dynamic change, folding and unfolding, becoming and becoming-nothing, subsuming extinctionality and subsumed materiality, nemocentric reality and phenomenal virtuality, territorialization, deterritorialization, and reterritorialization. In *Vibrant Matter,* Jane Bennett puts it this way: "By 'vitality' I mean the capacity of things — edibles, commodities, storms, metals — not only to impede or block the will and designs of humans but also to act as quasi agents or forces with trajectories, propensities, or tendencies of their own."[59]

In some sense, SA sees the delta as ontologically prior to its constituent parts. The change of territorialization (species' coming-into-being), deterritorialization (species' extinction), and reterritorialization (material analogy) is ontologically prior to the territory of species-being itself (assemblage-materiality).

SA's dark perversion is this: deterritorialization always has the upper-hand over reterritorialization. At the core of every assemblage-materiality is an unavoidable fragility, a tendency towards discontinuity, disparity, and extinction, a becoming-nothing at the core of every becoming-something — this is what it means for a species to be a species-towards-extinction. Cataclysm, annihilation, and extinction are the rules; assemblage, coming-together, and being-something are the strange, uncanny, antagonistic, and interruptive exceptions.

In *On an Ungrounded Earth,* Ben Woodard calls this "a materiality made of powers and flows and not objects, or at least not objects that are anything more than temporary arrests or slowing-down of those powers."[60] For Woodard, the existence of objects is nothing more than the "temporary arrests" or "slowing-down" of vitalistic "powers and flows"; it is an interruptive existence. E.g., the "temporary arrest" of an extinction-event is an interruption of the power/flow of extinctionality.

What does it mean to consider existence as existence *qua* interruption, i.e., existence as antagonistic? In 2.6, we considered this quotation from Schelling: "The product is originally nothing but a mere point, a mere limit, and it is only through Nature's battling against this point that it is, so to speak, raised to a full sphere, a product."[61] Schelling's "Nature" is constantly battling against existence — the "mere point" or "mere limit," and this battle is what makes a "product" of nature fully a product. For Schelling, there is a sense that existence is always existence *against* nature. Understanding existence as existence against nature is to understand existence as interruptive.

2. SA is both monistic and pluralistic.

In *A Thousand Plateaus*, Deleuze and Guattari write: "monism = pluralism."[62] For Deleuze and Guattari, the territorialization of cities — the way in which their constituent parts are assembled to form an identity — is an example of this. The city (a monad) is constituted by disparate but assembled parts (a plurality).

Following Deleuze and Guattari, SA is both monistic and pluralistic. The territorialization of an assemblage-materiality (the territory of species-being) is an example of this. An assemblage-materiality (a monad) is a disparate assemblage of artifact-materiality and embodiment-materiality (a plurality).

For Deleuze and Guattari, "monism = pluralism" is also true of becoming, which is immanent rather than transcendent, univocal. A monism of becoming is manifested in a pluralism of forces of becoming, i.e., there are a plurality of ways in which becoming happens and a plurality of forms that becoming might take. Similarly, SA's monism of becoming-extinct or unbecoming is manifested in a pluralism of forces: the deterritorialization of assemblage-materiality, annihilation, obliteration, extinction, decay, degeneration, rot, etc. Woodard helpfully terms this "rot-as-process."[63] SA is speculative demonology (plural) as a theodicy of putrefaction (univocal).

Hindu cosmogony provides an illuminating context for thinking about rot as both a pluralism and a monism. In Hindu cosmogony, the term "pralaya" refers to aeonic periods of disarray, dissolution, and decay. According to the Samkhya school of Hindu philosophy, these periods occur when the three "gunas" — i.e., the three major qualities of matter/nature/being — are in balance. The "balanced" state of things is thus seen to be a state of disarray and decomposition.

The *Vishnu Purana*, an ancient Hindu text, describes four categories of Pralaya: "The dissolution of all things is of four kinds; Naimittika, 'occasional'; Prákritika, 'elemental'; Atyantika, 'absolute'; Nitya, 'perpetual.'"[64] "Naimittika" is the night of Brahma, a period in which the universal monarch sleeps. This results in the dissolution of creatures, but not substances. "Prákritika" is a period in which Hiranyagarbha (the "mundane egg," the source of universal creation) dissolves and regresses back from whence it came; Prákritika is the great undo. "Atyantika" is the annihilation of the individual via Moksha, i.e., via a release from the cycle of birth and rebirth and therefore the assurance of futural nonexistence. "Nitya" is the extinction of life, the continuing apoptosis intrinsic to existence, constant and perpetual. Nitya refers to the death or annihilation of existing things. Pralaya is a monism in the sense that decay is singular and ontologically central, but a pluralism in the sense that a plurality of forces (or, in the case of Hindu cosmogony, temporalities/aeons) constitute decay.

3. SA collapses the organic/inorganic distinction. For SA, ontology is chemistry.

SA's monistic vision of becoming as becoming-extinct collapses the organic-inorganic distinction. All things —

organic and inorganic — are "animated" by rot and decay, by extinction and annihilation. The triumph of deterritorialization over assemblage is not unique to assemblage-materiality, but includes all material assemblages, organic and inorganic alike.

For SA, "material" or "stuff" is no longer so easily differentiated from "self" or "life" or "the vital." There are two reasons for this:

1. SA's nemocentrism collapses the phenomenal into the real (material, a carbon-based information-processing system). To distinguish between the material and the phenomenal is to distinguish between external reality and a representation of external reality. The phenomenal is understood as a material virtuality, and thus the phenomenal/real distinction is muddied. Even still, it might be argued that the vital/non-vital or organic/inorganic distinction can be upheld, see (2).

2. SA's monism does not allow differentiation between the organic and inorganic because annihilation is not picky. Recall that the temporal bifocals of common-sense and causal time led to an understanding of extinction as inevitable decay. This decay is indifferent to "vitality" or organic-ness. Cioran wrote that "the universal view melts things into a blur."[65] SA's monism melts the organic/inorganic distinction into a blur.

For SA, the ontological is the chemical. In *Cyclonopedia,* Reza Negarestani writes: "Chemistry starts from within, but its existence is registered on the surface; ontology is, so to speak, merely a superficial symptom of chemistry."[66] The forces of annihilation, decay, and disassembly are *chemical.* That is, becoming-extinct acts as an acidity against the fragility and decrepitude of assembly and existence.

The chemical allows us to think the indistinctiveness of the organic/inorganic, to see the animation of all things by rot and decay in action. Some vitalisms, such as Deleuzo-Guattarian vitalism, are essentially forms of bio-idealism. Deleuze and Guattari write:

An abstract machine is neither an infrastructure that is determining in the last instance nor a transcendental Idea that is determining in the supreme instance. Rather, it plays a piloting role. The diagrammatic or abstract machine does not function to represent, even something real, but rather constructs a real that is yet to come, a new type of reality.[67]

This idealism is a distinction and mutual dependence between material becomings that *cannot act but exist*, and immaterial ideas that *can act but do not exist*; it is the correlation resurfacing.[68] SA thinks chemically to escape this bio-idealism: the inorganic/organic distinction collapses because at the core of each is an animation by fetid putrefaction.

In *Dialectic of Enlightenment*, Horkheimer and Adorno write: "Humans believe themselves free of fear when there is no longer anything unknown. This has determined the path of demythologization, of enlightenment, which *equates the living with the nonliving* as myth has equated the nonliving with the living."[69] Mythology "equated the nonliving with the living," seeing the animate in the inanimate, hence the term "animism." In the account of *Dialectic of the Enlightenment*, enlightenment similarly "equates the living and nonliving," seeing the inanimate in the animate.

The account of the demystification of enlightenment in *Dialectic of Enlightenment* entails a remystification (for Deleuze and Guattari, deterritorialization entails a reterritorialization). The equation of the living with the nonliving is not total, but partial. That is, a reactionary mélange of phenomenologies, pseudo-sciences (religiously inflected and not), and mysticisms abound in the age of enlightenment, not despite it but because of it. "Every action has an equal and opposite reaction" — if enlightenment is the indistinction of the living/nonliving (viz., the living *as* the nonliving), then the reactionary mélange is the remnant of the living/nonliving and organic/inorganic distinction.

Enlightenment (understood as demystification) equates the living with the nonliving, but science's remystified foundations not only distinguish between the living and the nonliving but also reaffirm this distinction. We do not tend to conflate the phenomenal with the material — even a radical behaviorism acknowledges that the phenomenal is an inscrutable black box — but retain meaning or purpose as a reification of the "great chain of being." Adorno and Horkheimer write that "the disenchantment of the world means the extirpation of animism."[70] Science's re-enchantment of the world shows this extirpation to be unfinished, the animism of the human is not subject to the same annihilative collapse as the rest of the world-for-us. All critiques of enlightenment are critiques of incipient enlightenment or enlightenment overthrown.

The critique of enlightenment in *Dialectic of Enlightenment* is a critique of science's new context of signification, which provides the basis for "the culture industry" and the proliferation of mass media. This is a critique of the new meaning rather than a critique of enlightenment's unmeaning. Horkheimer and Adorno write: "On their way toward modern science human beings have discarded meaning."[71] We don't live in a nihilistic world, but remain solidly in a meaningful world, we find meaning in mass media, purpose in a suburban house with a white picket fence, and telos in a week or two of paid vacation. Horkheimer and Adorno are disquieted not by meaninglessness, but by this new meaning.

The demystification of the enlightenment is typified by "Thanatos," the Freudian death drive or death instinct, as the opposition to life, reproduction, sex, adaptation, positive transformation, and the like. The remystification that follows is typified by "Eros," the Freudian life drive or life instinct, as the assemblage of life, reproduction, sex, etc. — at odds with and in eternal opposition to Thanatos.

The reterritorialization of the world-for-us, here understood as a remystification, is the triumph (or, at least, partial triumph) of Eros over Thanatos. In *Eros and Civilization*, Marcuse writes that "the life instincts (Eros) gain ascendancy over the death instincts."[72] The Eros/Thanatos distinction is a reaffirmation of the living/nonliving, organic/inorganic distinction. Eros and Thanatos are persistently in conflict with one another; Marcuse tells us that Eros and Thanatos are the two basic instincts whose "ubiquitous presence and continuous fusion (and de-fusion) characterize the life process."[73] This is not just a "continuous fusion (and de-fusion)," but a subjugation of Thanatos by Eros. Marcuse, again: "Life is the fusion of Eros and the death instinct; in this fusion Eros has subdued its hostile partner."[74]

When Horkheimer and Adorno critique enlightenment (viz., incipient enlightenment, the overthrow of enlightenment), they are critiquing the subjugation of Thanatos by Eros and thus the remystified reification of the living/nonliving distinction. The new, capitalist *Weltanschauung* (worldview) that they find troubling is a Weltanschauung of the subjugation of Thanatos. We live in the moment, any futural thought in which we might engage consists primarily in vacation-planning and retirement-logistics, sex is not a means to an end but the point (i.e., a matter of acquisition), and money or power emerges as the new telos. Simply put, the problem is not the demystification of enlightenment but the *partial* demystification of enlightenment, enlightenment does not go far enough.

Absolute demystification is conceivable, it is the Metzingerian collapse of the phenomenal/real distinction, the engendering of Foucault's end. Nemocentrism collapses the phenomenal into the real (viz., material, a carbon-based information-processing system). To distinguish between the material and the phenomenal becomes to distinguish between external reality and a representation of external reality. The phenomenal is understood as a material virtuality and, *ipso facto*, the phenomenal/ real distinction is muddied.

The Metzingerian collapse is the subsumption of Eros under Thanatos. The interiority of implacable death (following Heidegger and Hägglund, see 2.5) is not merely a product of organic animation, of being qua being-alive, but of existence *as such*. The subsumption of Eros under Thanatos is thus an absolute demystification: the living/nonliving distinction is collapsed because fetid putrefaction, annihilation, and decay (Being-towards-death) are not anthropocentric but onto-genic, i.e., decay is the great equalizer. Becoming (in the sense of a process philosophy) is apoptosistic: a becoming-inorganic is intrinsic to every organic thing. The critique of enlightenment in *Dialectic of Enlightenment* is a critique of reterritorialization *against* apoptosistic becoming, rather than *of* apoptosistic becoming. Deterritorialization, though, is the prerogative of ontology and the new telos is thereby torn asunder by SA's chemistry.

4. SA is a meta-nihilism — a mad, black Levinasianism.

Let's consider an interesting objection to SA on ethical grounds: SA's ontological prioritization of decay and extinction over existence or assemblage leads to a nihilism. If one accepts SA's premise, nothing really matters anymore. Why should we, who find ourselves in the Holocene extinction, care about the preservation of existence if everything is doomed anyways?

SA does not entail a nihilism, but rather a meta-nihilism. If nihilism tells us that nothing matters and that existence and becoming are irrelevant or beyond consideration, SA's meta-nihilism tells us that the thing that matters *is* that nothing matters, that existence is always existence-against and becoming is always becoming-extinct.

We *should* care about the Holocene extinction, it does matter, because it so obviously tells us that nothing matters, that existence is interruptive and becoming is becoming-extinct. In *Nihil Unbound*, Brassier writes that "nihilism is not an existential quandary but a speculative opportunity."[75] SA's meta-nihilism is an *ethical opportunity*. In an age of extinctions, it makes sense to ground ethics in an ontology of becoming-extinct.

This ethics sees extinction as interruptive and becoming as annihilative, prioritizing questions of preservation. For SA, the predominant ethical questions concern whether it is right to prolong interruptive existence or to accelerate decay. The hard work of ethical decision making has to be made in light of the fact that nothing is static or savable or permanent, that there is no salvation and no shining light at the end of the tunnel.

The otherization (or, minimization, objectification) of rot which is integral both to a non-nihilism (things matter, there is meaning, rot defangs meaning) and non-meta-nihilism (nothing matters, there is no meaning, rot is an irrelevancy) leads to a view of being or existence as permanence rather than pure, negative delta. In this view, ethics is necrocratic: ethical consideration is chiefly granted to the *gone-but-should-have-stayed* or the *left-too-soon*. Mourning takes the place of living with the change or "staying with the trouble."[76] This view perceives decay as primarily *xenotic*, i.e., the Other decays while the self remains. This is simply an elaboration of the notion operating in the background of both non-nihilism and non-meta-nihilism: that there can be no existence without existents, that to exist is to exist iteratively. The encounter with the Other is, in this view, a making-Same of the Other. The encounter with the Other is here a process of making-Same; the Other must be rendered intelligible via a correlation with thought, context, the categories of understanding, knowledge, and so on. The Other can only exist insofar as they *exist for me* — that is, insofar as they are a particular existent seen through a particular lens to which they are correlated and from which they are inextricable.[77]

SA responds as a mad, black Levinasianism. This mad, black Levinasian ethic, in which the face to face encounter with the Other (understood as an Other which negates the organic/inorganic distinction) is prioritized not only ethically but in which the ontological *is* the ethical, the result of a reactionary movement contra the iterative nature of existence as existence-in-existents.[78] The Other remains the Other qua Other insofar as the existence of the Other is an existence unbridled by existents, unconstrained by iteration. At the core of the Other is an "other," an "*il y a*," or the "there is" — a being *as such*, an unthought and unthinkable being, a being beyond the correlation.

In *Existence and Existents*, Levinas writes:

The things of the day world then do not in the night become the source of the "horror of darkness" because our look cannot catch them in their "unforeseeable plots"; on the contrary, they get their fantastic character from this horror. Darkness... reduces them to undetermined, anonymous being, which they exude.[79]

Levinas' "anonymous being," also termed the "*il y a*" (i.e., the "there is"), is not exhaustible or given in the same sense as Heideggerian Being qua Dasein. Rather, it is an existence without an existent, a void of Being qua being qua nothingness. In its neutrality, the il y a is devoid of meaning. For Levinas, the face to face encounter with the Other exposes the il y a in a process of "hypostasis," i.e., a process of becoming-aware of the Other and the phenomenological naming of things for what they are. Hypostasis begins with disgust at the Other, or laziness and tiredness in the direction of the Other, followed by the enjoyment or consciousness of the Other. Hypostasis shifts or alters the il y a, but does not remove it.

For SA's meta-nihilism, the void or the nothing (particularly, a becoming-nothing) lies in the ontological fact that existence (understood as the primacy of decay) is always against existents (people, raindrops, giraffes, houses, books, etc.). In its neutrality, becoming-nothing is, like the il y a, devoid of meaning. The face to face encounter with this becoming-nothing — with the Other qua annihilativity or the putrefied-Other — exposes and renders the putrefied-Other meaningful. Meta-nihilistic hypostasis, following Levinas, proceeds through disgust at the Other's decay, or laziness and tiredness in the direction of the Other's decay, followed by the consciousness (and, conceivably, enjoyment) of the Other's putrefactive essence (i.e., the Other's value lies in an existence-against). Meta-nihilistic hypostasis shifts or alters becoming-nothing — meaninglessness becomes meaning *in* meaninglessness via a correlationist praxis — but does not remove the ontological primacy of that becoming-nothing. For SA, *ethics is first philosophy* because ontology is chemistry: the chemical decay of the Other issues a call or summons to a face to face encounter with the Other qua putrefied-Other. For Levinas, the face of the Other says "thou shalt not kill." For SA, the face of the putrefied-Other says "along with me, thou shalt become-nothing." The first word of the Other is inscribed in the Capuchin Crypt: "What you are now we used to be; what we are now you will be..." The central question of philosophy is thus "how am I to live in light of my becoming-nothing and the becoming-nothing of the Other?"

The response to the becoming-nothing of the Other must be asymmetrical. That is, the face to face encounter with the annihilativity of the Other leads to a self-abnegation; this is the ground for material analogy (see 5.3). The putrefied-Other is given priority vis-à-vis the self. This encounter and the "first abnegation" that follows are prior to, and — in some sense — constitutive of ontology itself .[80] The face to face encounter's ontological or "metaphysical" nature is such that it is not representable; that is, it is not reducible to or exhausted by any linguified account or phenomenological descriptive explanation. The particular encounter of the face to face interrupts or cuts through the consciousness of the everyday; it's temporality constitutes a pointing-out of the facticity of annihilative process (becoming-nothing, inextricable death, extinctionality, annihilativity, etc.) contra the ontology of intentional consciousness qua permanence or stasis.

The ethical response to the annihilation of the Other is here separate from a moral response insofar as it occurs as ontology; there is no liberation from the debt to the putrefied-Other. A look at the putrefied-Other is always already an acknowledgment of the Other, it is an acknowledgment of the chemical, of putrefaction as the essence of things, of the core of reality as negative process. The face of the putrefied-Other forbids us to ignore it and thus to be violent against it. Abnegation is the response of the self to the shared annihilativity of the Other; the Other's annihilativity is analogically proximate but demands an ethically asymmetrical response. That is, the decay of the Other which constitutes the putrefaction of the putrefied-Other is essentially inexhaustible.

Levinas writes: "If one could possess, grasp, and know the other, it would not be other."[81] The putrefied-Other is not possessable, graspable, or knowable — hence the need for material analogy to proceed analogically. The putrefied-Other at first appears as enmeshed or entangled, inseparable from the annihilative processes of ontology, but pierces or punctures rot itself and appears to us then as the face of the putrefied-Other. This instantly becomes a demand, a call, a summons, a commitment to self-abnegate, to open-up. Levinas calls this the "commandment of God in the face." It is the commandment of God qua putrefaction in the face of the annihilativity of the Other, the face of the putrefied-Other. The speculative annihilationist epistemically seeks similarity vis-à-vis the Other while also ethically engaging in self-abnegation vis-à-vis the Other.

SA's meta-nihilism encompasses not only ethical value, but also truth value. A meta-nihilistic conception of truth must reject truth theories of coherence, correspondence, and pragmatism. Coherence theories of truth entail coherence to a worldview which matters, contra the meta-nihilistic contention that the only thing that matters is that nothing matters (nothing understood as a becoming-nothing, an apoptosistic process of decay). Correspondence theories of truth entail a correspondence to the world, to some whole/universal to which a particular theory or set of data must correspond in order to be "true." Truth thus presupposes a being-in-the-world and the ability to know the world in its totality. If a totality is the criterion of truth, then that totality matters, contra the meta-nihilistic contention. Pragmatic theories of truth (at least, those which assign truth values with an eye towards the future rather than retroactively) become problematic at a societal level, as truth values inevitability become a matter of majoritarian consensus. In this sense, the majority's consensus matters, contra — again — the meta-nihilistic contention.

One solution is to give up on truth. In 1.1, we considered the "Nietzschean solution" in which truth values are replaced with aesthetic preferences. Against Nietzsche, we employed Brassier: "I consider myself a nihilist precisely to the extent that I refuse this Nietzschean solution and continue to believe in the difference between truth and falsity, reality and appearance. In other words, I am a nihilist precisely because I still believe in truth, unlike those whose triumph over nihilism is won at the cost of sacrificing truth."[82] If meta-nihilism is compatible with a belief in truth, what sort of truth does it entail?

If philosophy can be broadly construed as a project of truth-finding, it proceeds strangely. Central to theoretical discourse is the method of re-definition. Rather than objecting to a theory on its own terms, the philosopher often changes the terms, constructing a new theory which suits the new terms.

Philosophical history is not a history of theoretical succession, but of theoretical misreading. This misreading and re-definition results in the creation of new concepts. Deleuze and Guattari write that "the object of philosophy is to create concepts that are always new."[83] If philosophy is the creation of concepts, often proceeding by re-definition, which concepts are "true"?

SA's meta-nihilism tells us that the thing that matters is that nothing matters, i.e., the criterion for truth must be a becoming-nothing. This is not the abolition of truth, but the construction of truth qua demonology. The term "demonology" denotes the uncanniness of a coherence theory of truth which departs from the archetypal "natural order" or ontology. Meta-nihilistic truth is demonological insofar as it ascribes truth to coherence *against* that archetypal ontology, but rather coheres with annihilative processes.

The meaning of meaninglessness, the telos of meta-nihilism, is truth. Truth *just is* the result of meta-nihilistic thinking, it is absolute demystification, the subsumption of Eros under Thanatos. True concepts are true because they are the product of a heresy against life (the radicalization of Thanatos, contra Eros). Truth is the result of thought qua putrefied-thought, i.e., a thought that acknowledges the ontological centrality of deterioration and sees truth as a "correspondence" not with the world or the whole, but with the recalcitrance of rot.

SA's meta-nihilism allows for aesthetic value as well. In the traditional aesthetics of Japan, "wabi-sabi" (侘寂) denotes an aesthetic appreciation of impermanence, transience, decay, and incompleteness. Wabi-sabi emphasizes roughness, simplicity, and ordinariness. In "Wabi-sabi," Richard Martin writes that "wabi-sabi represents a comprehensive Japanese aesthetic focused on the acceptance of impermanence or transience...[it] speaks of a readiness to accept things as they are."[84] A nihilistic aesthetic — if such an aesthetic is not just a contradiction in terms — stops at "the way things are." SA's meta-nihilism "speaks of a readiness to accept" the way things are, it appreciates that the thing that matters is that nothing matters, that becoming is always becoming-nothing (decay) and existence is always existence-against (interruptive).

5. SA is speculative.

For SA, things in-themselves are there before us, but they are not *for us* — it is not a negative theology of process but an ontology of negative process. For Deleuze, the dynamic (or vital) is held captive within the idea, grounded by thought.[85] Becoming is thinking-becoming.

Following Deleuze, extinction becomes thinking extinction: extinction must be pre-thinkable. We have argued, though, that extinction entails the extinction of thought and thus cannot be pre-thinkable. It must be a real uncorrelated with thought.

Thought (or, the idea) faces two distinct disadvantages in regard to knowing the real: natural obfuscation and time. The archaeologist seeks to understand material history, but the archaeologist is nothing other than a carbon-based information-processing system with some degree of virtual phenomenality. It is symptomatic of human arrogance to imagine that the archaeologist can ever overcome nature's obfuscation. This is not to suggest that the archaeologist cannot begin to grasp nature (or things in-themselves, the real, etc.), but that the "whole picture" is always out of view.

The archaeologist must also contend with time: there are some elements of the past that are inaccessible. Time is a force of decay and this decay bolsters the "onto-epistemological indistinction" of material history.[86] Material rots, we rot — insofar as extinctionality is the potential for rotting, insofar as being a species-towards-extinction is synonymous with being a species-towards-rotting, rot-as-process is inextricable from species-being.

Thought, then, is not up to the task of knowing the real or

rendering nature pre-thinkable. Contra Deleuze, thought must *speculate* about the real, about the destruction of worlds. SA is speculative because it acknowledges that thought can only speculate about the uncorrelated real.

To say that our knowledge of the real is "speculative" is not to discount its epistemic validity. Archaeology is predicated on speculation. Epistemic ground — if the knowledge claimed refers to an uncorrelated real, unbridled by thought — must be speculative in nature, because the real is uncorrelated and thus not pre-thinkable. The face to face encounter with the putrefied-Other is a form of speculation which is an epistemically valid form of coming-to-know the Other through shared annihilativity, and is also a making primary of the first abnegation. This speculative encounter is not a possession, grasping, total knowledge, or power over the Other, but first and foremost an ethical call to abnegate the self vis-à-vis the Other. The inexhaustibility of the putrefied-Other makes possession or knowledge of or power over the Other unattainable. The unspeakable, speculative encounter with the putrefied-Other, with a shared annihilativity which results in ethical asymmetry (self-abnegation), is the epistemic ground of archaeological analysis.

In *Dialectic of Enlightenment*, Horkheimer and Adorno note that mathematics transforms the unknown (the real) into the "unknown quantity of an equation," the real/unknown is thus "made into something long familiar before any value has been assigned."[87] This is nature as pre-thinkable, the unknown is made known because it is granted a thinkable context of signification in which its unknowability can be contained and diluted. The ideology of pre-thinkability finds its roots in Kant. Horkheimer and Adorno write: "Kant combined the doctrine of thought's restlessly toilsome progress towards infinity with insistence on its insufficiency and eternal limitation...There is no being in the world that knowledge cannot penetrate, but what can be penetrated by knowledge is not being."[88] Pre-thinkability is thus an elaboration of the correlation: thought/knowledge is correlated with being, i.e., there can be no thought without being (thought-in-the-world), and being is correlated with thought/knowledge, i.e., being only *exists* insofar as it exists for us or insofar as it is thinkable. Being, therefore, is pre-thinkable because to be *just is* to be pre-thinkable. Comprehensibility is both thought's progress towards the absolute and thought's "eternal limitation."

SA disputes the correlation: being is radically un-pre-thinkable and thought can think (speculate) past or beyond being. Horkheimer and Adorno, again: "a true praxis capable of overturning the status quo depends on theory's refusal to yield to the oblivion in which society allows thought to ossify."[89] SA's speculation is this refusal, the untying or unchaining of thought from being such that a true archaeological praxis can overturn the status quo of archaeological theoretic approaches.

Walter Benjamin's "The Work of Art in the Age of Mechanical Reproduction" presents a case study of this speculation beyond being. Benjamin remarks that the advent of film "burst this prison-world asunder by the dynamite of the tenth of a second, so that now, in the midst of its far-flung ruins and debris, we calmly and adventurously go traveling."[90] This bursting open of the "prison-world" is film's speculative quality, i.e., the medium of film provides a framework for speculation.

Benjamin employs Dadaism as paradigmatic with respect to film's later speculation. He writes: "Dadaistic activities actually assured a rather vehement distraction by making works of art the center of scandal. One requirement was foremost: to outrage the public."[91] Dadaism is paradigmatic with respect to SA's speculation as well, at least insofar as it also aims "to outrage the public." There is a shocking eeriness or strangeness — an uncanniness — in SA's speculation: the uncorrelated real is a world-without-us[92] and a world of rot and putridity. As such, SA's speculation is *outraging* in much the same way as Dadaistic speculation: for each, the real is other because the real is not pre-thinkable.

For Kant (see 1.1), being is essentially tied to a praxis of self-reflection — this generates Meillassoux's correlation. For Hegel, the correlation is all-consuming inasmuch as being is tied instead to the labor of history — this transforms the correlation from an internality into an externality. Apropos of Hegel, Horkheimer said that the real (or, reality) "is seen by philosophy only as something rotten, which seems to exist but is not real in and for itself."[93] Hegel's real is not only pre-thinkable but is only real insofar as it can be conceived historically; the real is subsumed under the march/labor of history. SA's speculation can be thought of as altogether contra this Hegelian move. Dadaistic speculation decorrelates the real from self-reflection (Kant) and particularly from history or progress (Hegel). The real is thus seen to be unteleological, unprogressive, and an unfolding. Horkheimer, again: "Philosophy is therefore not a consolation; it is more: it reconciles, it transfigures, a reality that appears to be unjust, making it appear rational."[94] SA's speculation is not a consolation either, it is less: it does not reconcile or transfigure the real (no matter how "unjust" it might appear), but rather "stays with the trouble" of the real. Instead of rationalizing, it — to return to Benjamin — bursts open the "prison-world" of the correlation so that we can "calmly and adventurously go traveling" anew.

6. SA is ungrounded.

For archaeological statements regarding extinct species to be possible, our access to the real must be decoupled from a conception of ourselves as "selves." That is, access to the real must be seen to be inhuman. Ray Brassier describes it this way: the real is "a mind-independent reality, which, despite the presumptions of human narcissism, is indifferent to our existence and oblivious to the 'values' and 'meanings' which we would drape over it in order to make it more hospitable."[95]

Plotinus' "One" — which, for SA, takes the form of extinctions, interruptions, and inconsistencies — cannot be subject to subjects, not contextualized or linguified or culturalized, but must be understood as having no epistemic ground, i.e., it is ungrounded. Archaeology, as a science, must not "serve" us, it cannot "work for our betterment" — this would be a reification of the correlation — rather, it must be saprophytic/earthwormic — fueled by decay — and based on speculation about the un-pre-thinkable or ungrounded real.

In "Becoming Spice," Nicola Masciandaro writes:

The geophilosopher is one who philosophically experiences rather than flees the earth, who passes through by remaining with it. Geophilosophical experience entails facing, more and more deeply, the fact of earth as the place of philosophy, and more profoundly, experiencing earth as facticity itself, the site of thought's passage to the absolute.[96]

Our archaeological reorientation, too, "entails facing, more and more deeply, the fact of earth as the place of philosophy"; the un-pre-thinkable Earth becomes "the site of thought's passage to the absolute." Thought no longer makes, forms, or creates material history ("the earth"), but can only speculate. For Masciandaro, philosophy is predicated on the earth, not ontologically below the real but floating above it. For us, thought is predicated on dark flux, ontologically above rather than beneath that flux.

Negarestani tells us that "ungrounding is involved with discovering or unearthing a chemically-degenerating underside to the ground."[97] Following Negarestani, our ungrounding provides the ground for epistemic "discovering or unearthing." The ungrounding of the real from thought provides the ground for speculation. The encounter with the putrefied-Other is not "grounded" in the sense that it is outside of any linguistic context and is not subject to the categories of understanding, but rather lies firmly within the manifest itself. Material analogy (epistemic) and first self-abnegation (ethical/ontological) bridge the categories and the manifest via a dark, speculative encounter with the putrefied-Other.

6.4 Thought's extinction, capital, and the horizon of thought

How can thought understood as speculation think thought's extinction? Is there a force other than extinction about which we can speculate, allowing us to think thought's extinction in a tangible way?

The extinction of thought has three important criteria:

1. The extinction of thought is annihilative. It must entail violent disassembly and mass death.
2. The extinction of thought is abolitionist. Identity relies on thinking-identity. The Cartesian rational being proclaims the *cogito*: "I think, therefore I am." The extinction of thought is the extinction of "I am."
3. The extinction of thought is unknowable but thinkable. Knowing the extinction of thought is knowing the real unbridled by thought. This unbridled real is beyond our epistemic purview. That being said, there is difference between knowability and thinkability. We may never know the extinction of thought (see 1.4), but we can certainly speculate about it.

Is there a force other than extinction than meets these criteria? Let's consider capital:

1. Capital is annihilative. For Marx — it subsumes labor, for xenofeminist accelerationisms — it abolishes the injustices of

gender. In *General Intellects*, McKenzie Wark writes: "The machine system means…the replacement of labor by capital. Wealth can be created independently of labor time."[98] Capital cares only for its own propagation: "wealth can be created independently of labor time" — techno-mitosis. Negarestani, following Land, remarks that "the tortuous economy of dissipation inherent to capitalism" is its "partially repressed desire for meltdown."[99] Capitalism is not an economic state but an anti-essentialist set of processes which are techno-mitosistically dissipative and dissolutive in regard to stasis, at least insofar as said stasis stands in the way of radical commodification. Land, in "Machinic Desire":

Machinic desire can seem a little inhuman, as it rips up political cultures, deletes traditions, dissolves subjectivities, and hacks through security apparatuses, tracking a soulless tropism to zero control. This is because what appears to humanity as the history of capitalism is an invasion from the future by an artificial intelligent space that must assemble itself entirely from its enemy's resources.[100]

The inhumanity of capitalism (Deleuzo-Guattarian "machinic desire") is annihilative inasmuch as it is abolitionist or emancipative — "rips up political cultures, deletes traditions, dissolves subjectivities, etc." Negarestani notes that "capitalism is not a human symptom but rather a planetary inevitability. In other words, Capitalism was here even before human existence, waiting for a host."[101] This is because capitalism is a symptom of the petropolitical, lubricated — as it were — by the (bacterial) production of oil. It is quite literally inhuman —it's archaeo-bacterial chemistry or petropolitical microbiology.

2. Capital is abolitionist or emancipative. Capital's annihilativity is abolitionist insofar as techno-mitosis is prioritized over identity. In "Xenofeminism: A Politics for Alienation," Laboria Cuboniks

writes: "'Gender abolitionism' is shorthand for the ambition to construct a society where traits currently assembled under the rubric of gender, no longer furnish a grid for the asymmetric operation of power."[102] Capital abolishes gender as fodder for "the asymmetric operation of power" because it prioritizes techno-mitosistic process over "traits currently assembled under the rubric of gender." Propagation as such (and, often, self-propagation as such) becomes the arbiter of worth. Capital tends towards schizo-identity. Wark writes, contra Marx: "There is no eternal capital. It has no transhistorical essence. It mutates both in particulars and its abstract forms."[103] Not only is capital-in-itself a schizo-capital, but it also disorients *us* enough to render our own self-image strange, uncanny, horrific, and mechanistic. Our resultant schizo-identity is the beginning of the realization that each of us is a unit of labor subsumed by capital, that each of us is not so neatly differentiable from products and goods and items. For today's techno-science, the user is already the product.

3. Capital is unknowable: techno-mitosis is uncanny, like looking in the mirror expecting to see yourself and instead seeing a cog in some machinic identity-disassembly line. There is no one in charge and no one with the answers: capital is beyond intelligibility. Capital gets at the "great outdoors": it cannot be known. We speculate about it — this is what economists, politicians, futurists, and the like do — and in that regard it is thinkable. But it is not knowable.

Speculation about capital is possible: we can think capital, even if we cannot know capital. In the same way, speculation about the extinction of thought is possible, even if we cannot *know* the extinction of thought. Speculating about capital provides a model for SA's mad, black Levinasianism: we can think the extinction of thought because we can be with (come face to face with) the extinctionality/annihilativity of the Other qua putrefied-Other. Speculation about the extinction of thought *just is* the face to face encounter with putrefaction or annihilation in-itself via the particular facticity of annihilativity in the putrefied-Other.

The problematization of thought thinking thought's extinction relies on the notion that to think thought's extinction (non-thought) is to make non-thought into a thought and thus to think thought. The extinction of thought, then, cannot be thought. This problematization (viz., the "correlational circle") operates with too narrow a conception of "thought." Insofar as thought is a rational process through which certainty or knowledge is gained, thought's extinction is unthinkable. Insofar, though, as thought is understood as the being-with (the face to face encounter with) the Other, thinking thought's extinction is not only possible but a constant occurrence. To speculatively encounter the extinction of thought in this way is to encounter the extinctionality, annihilativity, or putrefaction of the Other. In the face of the putrefied-Other, we can see thought's extinction, because the end of putrefaction or the categorical annihilation of the putrefied-Other renders the encounter impossible, which is the horizon of thought. This horizon is discernible in the ceaseless encounter with the putrefied-Other.

6.5 The unheimlich real: existence without existents

We previously said that the history of Kantian and post-Kantian philosophy has been the history of a singular notion: there can be no existence without existents. That is, existence *as such* cannot exist uninstantiated; existence is always existence-of. Perhaps existence *as such* is the set of all existents, but it can be nothing outside of this set, nothing beyond, nothing infinite, nothing absolute. Existence (being) cannot be understood apart from existents (thinking beings, thought). We termed this the thesis of existentiality and found that archaeological theoretic approaches reformulate and reify this thesis.

The question at hand is this: can archaeological theory be reframed and reoriented such that the encounter with the Other is an encounter with the Other qua Other, sans a making-Same? That is, can archaeology be grounded on a theoretic basis other than the thesis of existentiality? Can a thesis of non-existentiality be formulated?

This thesis must address both the thesis of human finitude and the thesis of access. In regard to the former, the in-itself must be understood outside of a for-us; i.e., there must be an in-itself (an existence or being) which is understandable without subsumption under the categories of understanding. It must be possible to think conceptually without thinking in concepts. In regard to the latter, the world/world relation must be understood apart from the human/world relation, to think the world/world relation must not subsume that relation under the categories of understanding and thus under the human/world relation. That is to say, there must be a way to understand existence without existents in a non-iterative abstraction that can ground the encounter with the Other sans a making-Same of the Other. This encounter must be non-sympathetic; that is, it must rely totally on aberration and distinction, rather than commonality or analogy, (un)likeness or commensurability. This encounter is not a matter of empathetic "I see my self in You" or a relation to the Other grounded in common experience; it is the radical way in which the self and the Other — each unrelated and un-relatable in-itself, each entirely alone in its being qua being — can *be-with* each other. To *explain* or *understand* (in thought) the disparity between beings is to explain it away, to miss the point. The Other cannot be grasped or known or possessed; to see the Other as the Other, the Other qua Other, is necessarily to be-with the Other and to do nothing besides. The Other, in this sense, can only be encountered, met, greeted, welcomed. The Other can only be seen in its immediacy, in its raw ontology, in its face, in its anonymity.

When we think the extinction of thought — when we engage in speculation or when we come face to face with the putrefied-Other — what do we think, what do we come face to face with? Our speculation must get at the real uncoupled from thought (or culture, language, history, mode, etc.). What would this real be like?

Consider Eugene Thacker, who writes: "if absolute extinction implies that there can be no thought of extinction, then this thought in-itself leaves but one avenue open: that extinction can only be thought, that it can only be said to exist, as a *speculative annihilation*...Extinction is a void."[104]

Also consider David Peak: "Horror...is the permission to speculate beyond our own limitations as a species."[105] The extinction of thought is "beyond our own limitations as a species." In order to think thought's extinction, our speculation has to engage in speculative annihilation or what is more commonly termed "speculative horror." There is an abyss always out of view (the extinction of thought), about which we can only speculate, and this speculation renders the abyss horrific. Peak: "Horror overcomes the impossible by providing answers...in response to speculation."[106]

Thacker helpfully enumerates three distinct worlds which shed further light on the project of speculative horror: the world-for-us, the world-in-itself, and the world-without-us. For Thacker, the "world-for-us" is the world which is the product of philosophies of access and philosophies of human finitude, it is the world which this project seeks to problematize because it renders statements about extinct species incoherent. The "world-in-itself," the "real," is outside of our purview, behind an impenetrable epistemic wall; it is an inaccessible abyss. This is the world of physics and the natural sciences, it is Sellars' "scientific image" of man-in-the-world, detached from and irreconcilable with the "manifest image of man-in-the-world." It is the world of the extinction of thought, it is the world of capital's degenerative techno-mitosis and discordant schizo-identity. The "world-without-us" is the world-for-us subtracted from the world-in-itself. Thacker writes: "the world-without-us allows us to think the world-in-itself...the world-without-us is the subtraction of the human from the world."[107] This is the world of enlightenment properly construed, the world of an unbridled speculation which calls into question all beliefs; it is an inhuman, unheimlich world.

"Unheimlich," here, is a (dis)adaptation of the Freudian term. In his essay, "The Uncanny," Freud uses the term to denote that which is strangely familiar in a way that is unhomely, unsettling, eerie, weird, taboo, uncomfortable, or disgusting.[108] For our purposes, "unheimlich" refers to the unsettling horror of the real, the realization of the annihilative, dynamic forces at play. The unheimlich real is, thus, the speculative real of our "annihilationism," it is the place to which speculation about the extinction of thought leads.

The unheimlich real is fundamentally an elaboration of Levinas' "*il y a,*" or anonymous being — the "there is," the existence without existents. For Levinas, the il y a entails an experience of horror and, notably, an experience that is unspeakable and unknowable. It can only be accessed by speculation (viz., as the encounter with the Other), and speaking it or perhaps even thinking it grants the existence an existent and thus fogs or clouds the il y a *in-itself.* The extinction of thought and the continuation of being *is* the il y a, it is the survival of existence *sans* existents. In that sense, it can be encountered face to face — but the speaking of it, thinking of it, knowing of it, grasping of it, or possessing of it is always an anthropomorphism, a paraphrasing in human terms. The il y a, existence without existents, being uncoupled from and uncorrelated with thought, can only be encountered face to face. This encounter with the il y a is always an encounter with a particular manifestation of il y a, an existence *sans* existent at the core of every existent, a becoming-nothing interior to every becoming-something; i.e., it is encountered in the face to face with a *particular* putrefied-Other.

Being is here not correlated with thought or taxonomy — the manifest is not correlated with the categories of understanding — to the extent that being is in excess of all categories, radicalizing them from within and blowing them apart, so to speak. Any categorizing praxis is always a simplifying (and a problematically simplifying) reductionism, at least inasmuch as being qua being escapes any sort of reductionist (viz., categorizing or taxonomic) account. In a sense, this is the primacy of the ontic over the ontological (beings before Being), but also a radicalizing of the ontic such that the unspeakability of the ontological is seen to be in excess of (and, thus, not neatly correlated with) the ontic. Being is multivocal, a pluralism, but also — essentially — a monism, even if it is an unspeakable, unknowable, monism. This epistemic wall, this unknowability, is not a total incommensurability: speculation (encountering) is by the very fact of the multivocality of being rendered the only possibility. *Speculation is ipso facto the way out of the thesis of existentiality.* The categories do not subsume the real because the real is in excess of them, but the categories also *do* exist, the real is not just accessible in the sense of a naïve realism. There is, rather, an in-between: a way to get to being qua being (a realism) and also a way that is not a knowing of being qua being (not a naïve realism), but is instead a *speculative realism* which both does not privilege existents over existence and also does not claim that existence as such is available to us in its "totality."

The il y a is a sign detached from its context of signification, a Deleuzo-Guattarian deterritorialization of existents leaving behind only existence, being uncorrelated from thought. Material analogy proceeds via hypostasis; that is, material analogy reterritorializes the being or existence of the existent, the Other, via analogical analysis. On the other hand, speculation (viz., the face to face encounter with the Other) leaves existence detached from existents. The sign is detached from its context of signification in such a way that the sign can be a sign as it is in-itself. In this sense, the encounter is the end of enlightenment; it is a total deterritorialization, a demystification *sans* remystification, prior to remystification. Speculation is therefore necessarily prior to material analogy, hypostasis relies on the prior occurrence of the face to face encounter. The "outside" of pre-critical thought, the absolute, is found in the space between the self and the putrefied-Other, in between me and you, us and them. The exteriority that is the real takes the shape of space-between, being-with; that is, of the encounter. In the encounter, I see the il y a, the unheimlich real, at the core of the Other — I see the Other qua putrefied-Other and know it to be the real, the absolute, the outside, the manifest.

SA, which is based upon a *thesis of non-existentiality* — as a dark perversion of the encounter with the Other — speculates (encounters) the Other's essence as one of putrefaction, a tendency towards annihilation, an integral extinctionality. The encounter with the existent Other reveals the essence of that Other to be an existence *sans* existents, a dark flux interior to each instantiation of "permanence" or "stasis." This is the dark perversion of the encounter with the Other, or the imagination beyond particulation and towards excess, which allows for the speculation (encountering) of the Other's essence as anonymous being all the way down, beneath every iterative being. The thesis of non-existentiality is a re-grounding of archaeological theory which allows the *manière d'être* of being qua beings to shine forth, predicated on the encounter with the Other qua Other sans any making-Same of the Other.

Any praxis of iteration — that is, of recognizing the existent which exists (e.g., material analogy, hypostasis) — relies upon a prior encounter with existence as such, *sans* existents. This is an encounter with uncorrelated being, with chemical annihilativity as ontology, with the il y a. Archaeology, proceeding via material analogy, must be predicated on this encounter. NB: material analogy as a form of hypostasis is predicated upon the encounter with being *as such*, with the il y a.

To speculate about (i.e., to encounter) the unheimlich real is to speculate about the extinction of thought — it is to speculate about the "world-in-itself" by speculating about the "world-without-us." The world-without-us, the unheimlich real, existence without existents, is unsettling because it reveals material history to be a chemical, backwards-origami, unteleological, meta-nihilistic process of becoming-extinct/becoming-nothing. The unheimlich real is what is seen or felt, it is what we are being-with, in the face to face encounter with the putrefied-Other. It is the expression on the face of the Other.

Where does archaeology fit in? Can we say that the Australopithecus who made or used the artifacts at Lomekwi 3 is *extinct*?

SA's unground (viz., the encounter with the putrefied-Other and the self-abnegation and material analogy that follow successively) provides the ground for speculation about the extinction of thought: this speculation is an encountering of the unheimlich real. SA ontologically grounds speculation about the extinction of thought in the unspeakable encounter with the putrefied-Other, and thus grounds speculation about the extinction of Australopithecus. An ontological reorientation allows archaeology to speculate about thought's extinction, to be-with the uncorrelated real, granting archaeological statements about extinct species truth values, where before there were only contexts, cultures, and languages. While the encounter may be unspeakable in its totality, speculation (via material analogy) allows shared annihilativity to be communicated about the Other qua putrefied-Other and thus to be true *as such*.

Material analogy, which is the method of speculative annihilationist archaeology, is a shout in the void, "*a tale told by an idiot, full of sound and fury, signifying nothing,"*[109] not because anthropomorphism and the correlation are all-encompassing or that *"there is nothing outside of the text,"*[110] but because nearly everything is outside of the text, because the Other is subject to material history, which is a rapidly unfolding chemical/ontological process of putrefaction and decay. And yet, we do not give up on truth. We do not say that "there is nothing outside of the text" but understand explanation by anthropomorphism to be an explaining away. Instead, we do what we can, albeit against "onto-epistemological indistinction," to reorient ourselves to a world of the dark flux, annihilative transformation, interruptive existence, and perpetual extinction which characterizes material history such that we can come face to face with the unheimlich real of the putrefied-Other — the il y a — to talk of extinction where before there was only interpretive noise.

Notes

1. Harmand, Sonia, et al. "3.3-million-year-old Stone Tools from Lomekwi 3, West Turkana, Kenya." *Nature* 521 (May 21, 2015): 310–315. Accessed April 6, 2018. doi:10.1038/nature14464.

2. Johnson, Matthew. *Archaeological Theory: An Introduction.* Oxford: Blackwell Publishers, 1999, p. 103.

3. Johnson, Matthew. *Archaeological Theory: An Introduction.* Oxford: Blackwell Publishers, 1999, p. 102.

4. Feyerabend, Paul. *Against Method.* London and New York: Verso, 1988, p. 151.

5. Johnson, Matthew. *Archaeological Theory: An Introduction.* Oxford: Blackwell Publishers, 1999, p. 102.

6. Ibid., p. 102.

7. Webster, Gary S., R.A. Bentley, H.D.G Maschner and C. Chippindale, eds. "Culture history: a culture-historical approach." *Handbook of Archaeological Theories.* AltaMira Press, 2008, p. 12.

8. Feyerabend, Paul. *Against Method.* London and New York: Verso, 1988, p. 32.

9. Ibid., p. 32.

10. Nietzsche, Friedrich. 1901 (1968). *The Will to Power.* New York: Vintage Books. p. 267.

11. Brassier, Ray. *Nihil Unbound: Enlightenment and Extinction.* Basingstoke, Hampshire: Palgrave Macmillan, 2007, p. 206.

12. Brassier, Ray, and Marcin Rychter. "I Am a Nihilist Because I Still Believe in Truth." *Kronos* (March), 2011. Emphasis added.

13. Meillassoux, Quentin. *After Finitude: An Essay on the Necessity of Contingency.* Translated by Ray Brassier. London: Bloomsbury Academic, 2017, p. 5.

14. Meillassoux, Quentin. *After Finitude: An Essay on the*

Necessity of Contingency. Translated by Ray Brassier.
London: Bloomsbury Academic, 2017, p. 7.

15. Meillassoux, Quentin. *After Finitude: An Essay on the Necessity of Contingency.* Translated by Ray Brassier. London: Bloomsbury Academic, 2017, p. 9.

16. Johnson, Matthew. *Archaeological Theory: An Introduction.* Oxford: Blackwell Publishers, 1999, p. 102.

17. Schrödinger, Erwin. "Die gegenwärtige Situation in der Quantenmechanik (The present situation in quantum mechanics)." *Naturwissenschaften.* 23 (48), pp. 807–812.

18. Heidegger, Martin. *Being and Time.* Translated by John Macquarrie and Edward Robinson. Oxford, UK: Blackwell Publishers, 1962, p. 255.

19. Feyerabend, Paul. *Against Method.* London and New York: Verso, 1988, p. 50.

20. Feyerabend, Paul. *Against Method.* London and New York: Verso, 1988, pp. 27–28.

21. Lamport, Leslie. "Time, Clocks, and the Ordering of Events in a Distributed System." *Communications of the ACM* 21, no. 7 (1978): 558–565. doi:10.1145/359545.359563. This thought experiment is inspired by Lamport's model of "logical time." My "causal time" differs in several ways from Lamport's model, but retains the centrality of the causal connection.

22. Meillassoux, Quentin. *After Finitude: An Essay on the Necessity of Contingency.* Translated by Ray Brassier. London: Bloomsbury Academic, 2017, p. 33.

23. Ibid., p. 33.

24. Ibid., p. 33.

25. Ibid., p. 53.

26. Brassier, Ray, and Marcin Rychter. "I Am a Nihilist Because I Still Believe in Truth." *Kronos* (March), 2011.

27. Thomson, William. "On the Age of the Sun's Heat." *Lord Kelvin | On the Age of the Sun's Heat,* zapatopi.net/kelvin/papers/on_the_age_of_the_suns_heat.html#fn1.

28. Brassier, Ray. *Nihil Unbound: Enlightenment and Extinction.* Basingstoke, Hampshire: Palgrave Macmillan, 2007, p. 223. Emphasis added.
29. van Dooren, Thom. *Flight Ways: Life and Loss at the Edge of Extinction.* New York: Columbia University Press, 2014, p. 12.
30. Woodard, Ben. *On an Ungrounded Earth: Towards a New Geophilosophy.* Brooklyn, NY: Punctum Books, 2013, p. 15.
31. Ibid., p. 15.
32. Heidegger, Martin. *Being and Time.* Translated by John Macquarrie and Edward Robinson. Oxford, UK: Blackwell Publishers, 1962, p. 426.
33. Bergson, Henri, and W. Scott Palmet. *Matter and Memory.* Translated by Nancy Margaret Paul. NY: Zone Books, 1988, p. 17. Emphasis added.
34. Hägglund, Martin. *Radical Atheism: Derrida and the Time of Life.* Stanford: Stanford University Press, 2008, p. 19.
35. Negarestani, Reza. *Cyclonopedia: Complicity with Anonymous Materials.* Melbourne: Re.press, 2008, p. 17.
36. Schelling, F.W.J. *First Outline of a System of the Philosophy of Nature.* Translated by Keith R. Peterson. Albany: State University of New York Press, 2004, pp. 205–206.
37. Schelling, F.W.J. *First Outline of a System of the Philosophy of Nature.* Translated by Keith R. Peterson. Albany: State University of New York Press, 2004, p. 18.
38. Darwin, Charles. "Darwin 1859 Chapter II, p. 59." darwin-online.org.uk. 1859. Archived from the original on 21 October 2012. Retrieved 25 November 2012, p. 59.
39. Nagel, Thomas. "What Is It Like to Be a Bat?" *The Philosophical Review* 83, no. 4 (October 1974): 435–450. Accessed April 5, 2018. https://warwick.ac.uk/fac/cross_fac/iatl/activities/modules/ugmodules/humananimalstudies/lectures/32/nagel_bat.pdf, p. 441.
40. Kant, Immanuel. *Critique of Pure Reason.* Edited by Paul

Guyer and Allen W. Wood. Cambridge: Cambridge University Press, 1998, p. 359.

41. Heidegger, Martin. *Being and Time*. Translated by John Macquarrie and Edward Robinson. Oxford, UK: Blackwell Publishers, 1962, p. 255.

42. Metzinger, Thomas. *Being No One: The Self-Model Theory of Subjectivity*. Cambridge, Mass.; London: MIT Press, 2003, p. 1.

43. Ibid., p. 551.

44. Ibid., p. 557.

45. Ibid., p. 563.

46. Dōgen. *Shobogenzo Zuimonki*. Compiled by Ejō. Translated by Reiho Masunaga. New Edition. Honolulu, HI: University of Hawaii Press, 1975, III, p. 3. Emphasis added.

47. Brassier, Ray, and Bram Ieven. "Against an Aesthetics of Noise." *NY Web*, NY, www.ny-web.be/ transitzone/against-aesthetics-noise.html.

48. Meillassoux, Quentin. *After Finitude: An Essay on the Necessity of Contingency*. Translated by Ray Brassier. London: Bloomsbury Academic, 2017, p. 7.

49. Metzinger, Thomas. *Being No One: The Self-Model Theory of Subjectivity*. Cambridge, Mass.; London: MIT Press, 2003, p. 563.

50. Foucault, Michel. *The Order of Things*. London: Taylor and Francis E-Library, 2005. Accessed April 9, 2018. https://is.muni.cz/el/1423/jaro2013/SOC911/um/ Michel_Foucault_The_Order_of_Things.pdf, p. 422.

51. Hume, David. *A Treatise of Human Nature*. Edited by L.A. Selby-Bigge. Clarendon Press: Oxford, 1896. Accessed April 18, 2018. https://people.rit.edu/wlrgsh/HumeTreatise.pdf, pp. 244–245.

52. Brassier, Ray. *Nihil Unbound: Enlightenment and Extinction*. Basingstoke, Hampshire: Palgrave Macmillan, 2007, p. 3.

53. Sellars, Wilfrid. "Philosophy and the Scientific Image of

Man." *Empiricism and the Philosophy of Mind*, 1963, 1–40. Accessed April 6, 2018. doi:10.18411/a-2017-023. p. 6.

54. Ibid., p. 17.

55. Brassier, Ray. *Nihil Unbound: Enlightenment and Extinction.* Basingstoke, Hampshire: Palgrave Macmillan, 2007, p. 7.

56. Negarestani, Reza. "Drafting the Inhuman: Conjectures on Capitalism and Organic Necessity." In Levi R. Bryant, Nick Srnicek and Graham Harman (eds.), *The Speculative Turn: Continental Materialism and Realism.* 2011, p. 182.

57. van Dooren, Thom. *Flight Ways: Life and Loss at the Edge of Extinction.* New York: Columbia University Press, 2014, p. 27.

58. van Dooren, Thom. *Flight Ways: Life and Loss at the Edge of Extinction.* New York: Columbia University Press, 2014, pp. 38–39.

59. Bennett, Jane. *Vibrant Matter: A Political Ecology of Things.* Durham and London: Duke University Press, 2010, p. viii.

60. Woodard, Ben. *On an Ungrounded Earth: Towards a New Geophilosophy.* Brooklyn, NY: Punctum Books, 2013, p. 28.

61. Schelling, F.W.J. *First Outline of a System of the Philosophy of Nature.* Translated by Keith R. Peterson. Albany: State University of New York Press, 2004, pp. 205–206.

62. Deleuze, Gilles, and Félix Guattari. *A Thousand Plateaus.* Minneapolis: University of Minnesota Press, 2007, p. 20.

63. Woodard, Ben. *On an Ungrounded Earth: Towards a New Geophilosophy.* Brooklyn, NY: Punctum Books, 2013, p. 17.

64. Wilson, Horace Hayman, trans. *Vishnu Purana.* London: John Murray, 1840. Accessed April 28, 2018. http://cincinnatitemple.com/downloads/VishnuPurana.pdf, p. 132.

65. Cioran, E.M. *A Short History of Decay.* Translated by Richard Howard. New York: Arcade Publishing, 1949, p. 43.

66. Negarestani, Reza. *Cyclonopedia: Complicity with Anonymous Materials.* Melbourne: Re.press, 2008, p. 187.

67. Deleuze, Gilles, and Félix Guattari. *A Thousand Plateaus*. Minneapolis: University of Minnesota Press, 2007, p. 142.
68. Deleuze, Gilles, and Félix Guattari. *What Is Philosophy?* London: Verso, 2015, p. 213.
69. Horkheimer, Max, and Theodor W. Adorno. *Dialectic of Enlightenment: Philosophical Fragments*. Stanford, CA: Stanford University Press, 2002, p. 11. Emphasis added.
70. Horkheimer, Max, and Theodor W. Adorno. *Dialectic of Enlightenment: Philosophical Fragments*. Stanford, CA: Stanford University Press, 2002, p. 2.
71. Horkheimer, Max, and Theodor W. Adorno. *Dialectic of Enlightenment: Philosophical Fragments*. Stanford, CA: Stanford University Press, 2002, p. 3.
72. Marcuse, Herbert. *Eros and Civilization*. Boston, MA: Beacon Press, 1966, p. 25.
73. Ibid., p. 27.
74. Ibid., p. 27.
75. Brassier, Ray. *Nihil Unbound: Enlightenment and Extinction*. Basingstoke, Hampshire: Palgrave Macmillan, 2007, p. xi.
76. The phrase "staying with the trouble" is taken from Donna J. Haraway's *Staying with the Trouble: Making Kin in the Cthulucene*.
77. Heidegger, Martin. *Being and Time*. Translated by John Macquarrie and Edward Robinson. Oxford, UK: Blackwell Publishers, 1962, p. 255.
78. Levinas, Emmanuel. *The Levinas Reader*. Edited by Sean Hand. Oxford: Basil Blackwell, 1989, p. 39.
79. Levinas, Emmanuel. *Existence and Existents*. Translated by Alphonso Lingis. The Hague and Boston: Martinus Nijhoff, 1978, p. 54.
80. Levinas, Emmanuel. *The Levinas Reader*. Edited by Sean Hand. Oxford: Basil Blackwell, 1989, p. 39.
81. Ibid., p. 51.
82. Brassier, Ray, and Marcin Rychter. "I Am a Nihilist Because

I Still Believe in Truth." *Kronos* (March), 2011.

83. Deleuze, Gilles, and Félix Guattari. *What Is Philosophy?* London: Verso, 2015, p. 5.

84. Martin, Richard. "Wabi-sabi." Pepperdine University. Accessed April 22, 2018. http://dt.pepperdine.edu/courses/ greatbooks_v/gbv_101/Wabi-%20Sabi.PDF, p. 1.

85. Deleuze. *Difference and Repetition.* Translated by Paul Patton. New York: Columbia University Press, 1994, pp. 218–219.

86. Woodard, Ben. *On an Ungrounded Earth: Towards a New Geophilosophy.* Brooklyn, NY: Punctum Books, 2013, p. 16.

87. Horkheimer, Max, and Theodor W. Adorno. *Dialectic of Enlightenment: Philosophical Fragments.* Stanford, CA: Stanford University Press, 2002, p. 18.

88. Ibid., p. 19.

89. Ibid., p. 33.

90. Benjamin, Walter. "The Work of Art in the Age of Mechanical Reproduction." In *Illuminations: Essays and Reflections,* 1–32. Shocken Books, 1969, p. 22.

91. Ibid., p. 23.

92. The "world-without-us" is Eugene Thacker's concept. See 6.5 for an elaboration of this.

93. Horkheimer, Max. "The State of Contemporary Social Philosophy and the Tasks of a Institute for Social Research." In *Critical Theory and Society,* 25–36. New York, NY: Routledge, 1989, p. 27.

94. Ibid., p. 26.

95. Brassier, Ray. *Nihil Unbound: Enlightenment and Extinction.* Basingstoke, Hampshire: Palgrave Macmillan, 2007, p. xi.

96. Masciandaro, Nicola. "Becoming Spice." *Collapse* VI: 20v57, p. 28.

97. Negarestani, Reza. *Cyclonopedia: Complicity with Anonymous Materials.* Melbourne: Re.press, 2008, p. 43.

98. Wark, McKenzie. *General Intellects: Twenty-One Thinkers for the Twenty-First Century.* London: Verso, 2017, p. 12.

99. Negarestani, Reza. "Drafting the Inhuman: Conjectures on Capitalism and Organic Necessity." In Levi R. Bryant, Nick Srnicek and Graham Harman (eds.), *The Speculative Turn: Continental Materialism and Realism*. 2011, p. 184.

100. Land, Nick. "Machinic Desire." *Textual Practice* 7, no. 3 (2008): 471–482. doi:10.1080/09502369308582177, p. 479.

101. Negarestani, Reza. *Cyclonopedia: Complicity with Anonymous Materials*. Melbourne: Re.press, 2008, p. 27.

102. Laboria Cuboniks. "Xenofeminism: A Politics for Alienation." Accessed April 16, 2018. http://www.laboriacuboniks.net/20150612-xf_layout_web.pdf, 0x0E.

103. Wark, McKenzie. *General Intellects: Twenty-One Thinkers for the Twenty-First Century*. London: Verso, 2017, p. 13.

104. Thacker, Eugene. *In the Dust of This Planet*. Winchester: Zero Books, 2011, p. 125.

105. Peak, David. *The Spectacle of the Void*. USA: Schism Press, 2014, p. 93.

106. Ibid., p. 92.

107. Thacker, Eugene. *In the Dust of This Planet*. Winchester: Zero Books, 2011, pp. 4–6.

108. Freud, Sigmund. "The Uncanny." *Imago* Bd., V. (1919). Accessed April 8, 2018. doi:10.1037/ e417472005-415.

109. Shakespeare, William. *Macbeth*. Accessed April 07, 2018. http://www.folgerdigitaltexts.org/ html/Mac.html, 5.5.26-28.

110. Derrida, Jacques. *Of Grammatology*. Translated by Gayatri Chakravorty Spivak. Baltimore: Johns Hopkins University Press, 1974, p. 158.

Glossary

Annihilativity: see "extinctionality."

Apoptosistic: The interiority of Being-towards-death to Dasein, the inextricable core of being as a tendency towards degeneration.

Bio-idealism: A distinction and mutual dependence between material becomings that cannot act but exist, and immaterial ideas that can act but do not exist. The Deleuzo-Guattarian version of the correlation.

Correlation, correlationism: The statement *"z is"* means *"z is the correlate of thinking-z."* Thinking-z, or z-as-it-appears to me, is the only possibility for access. The correlation rather than each element (thought distinct from being) is the only thing that is accessible. The Kantian and post-Kantian conceit that being is coupled and correlated with thought such that neither can be understood separately.

Culturalization: The correlation of being to thought as the particular correlation of being to culture.

Dasein: Being, not restricted to humans as in Heidegger or certain animals but rather the state of existence of all things. In this sense, a chair is Being-towards-death (towards the annihilation of the chair) in the same way as a human is towards death.

Eros: The Freudian life drive or life instinct.

Extinctionality: Extinction in causal time, the inextricability of extinction from species-being, and the inevitability of extinction.

Il y a: Levinas' notion of existence without existents, the "there is" or the "anonymous being."

Levinasian(-ism): The philosophy of Emmanuel Levinas, particularly the formulation of the "face to face encounter with the Other" and the idea that ethics is either constitutive of or prior to ontology.

Linguistification: The correlation of being to thought as the particular correlation of being to language.

Meta-nihilism: The thing that matters is that nothing matters. Value is predicated on becoming-nothing, degeneration, and decay.

Monism: There is one type of thing. Particularly, process is singular and all categories or forces of process are reducible to a singular overarching process of decay.

Necrocratic: The prioritization or over-valuation of the dead or the extinct.

Nemocentrism: The theoretic view of Thomas Metzinger, the idea that the phenomenal is a representation of external reality for a carbon-based information-processing system.

Onto-genesis: Generated or caused by the state of things, by existence or reality.

Phenomenality: The phenomenal, subjective, or "inner" experience of being.

Philosophies of access: Theoretic approaches that privilege the human-world or self-real relation over other relations.

Philosophies of human finitude: Theoretic approaches that hold that the finitude of human experience is the horizon of thought. There is no such thing as absolute truth and we cannot think the absolute.

Pluralism: There are many types of things. Particularly, processes are multifaceted and irreducible to a singular overriding process.

Quasi-Australopithecus: The version of Australopithecus created by the correlation.

Remystification: The Deleuzo-Guattarian "reterritorialization" of enlightenment's demystification ("deterritorialization").

Schizo-identity: The identity that results from the subsumption of the individual under capital's techno-mitosis, the collapse of the phenomenal/real distinction within the self.

Self-abnegation: The ethically asymmetrical response to coming face to face with the Other. The Other is given priority vis-à-vis the self.

Speculative annihilationism (SA): The ontological view presented in the text.

Speculation: In this text, speculation is Levinas' face to face encounter with the Other, which is necessarily outside of any context, including linguistic or cultural context.

Subsumption: For Kant, the relation between the categories of understanding and the manifest: x is subsumed under y such that x is a manifestation or iteration of y and nothing besides.

Techno-mitosis: The process by which capital self-replicates, grows, and expands its territory.

Thanatos: The Freudian death drive or death instinct.

The earthwormic dialectic: Deleuzo-Guattarian "territorialization," "reterritorialization," and "deterritorialization," as applied to archaeology.

The face to face encounter with the Other (*rapport de face à face*): Levinas' notion of the encounter with the Other as constitutive of or primary to ontology.

The principle of sufficient reason: Every effect has a sufficient and theoretically discoverable cause or set of causes.

The putrefied-Other: The core or essence of putrefaction or annihilation within Levinas' Other. The annihilativity of the Other.

The real: being detached from thought, the absolute "outside" of pre-critical thought, the sign detached *in toto* from its context of signification.

Theory-ladenness: The idea that the discovery, use, or presentation of facts presupposes theoretical assumptions.

Virtual: A representational construct. For instance, Metzinger's conception of phenomenal is as a virtuality of the real.

Vitalism, dynamism: An ontology which prioritizes process over stasis or permanence, a "process ontology."

Xenoticization, xenotic: An otherization with negative connotations, the making-alien of the Other.

zero
books

CULTURE, SOCIETY & POLITICS

Contemporary culture has eliminated the concept and public figure of the intellectual. A cretinous anti-intellectualism presides, cheer-led by hacks in the pay of multinational corporations who reassure their bored readers that there is no need to rouse themselves from their stupor. Zer0 Books knows that another kind of discourse – intellectual without being academic, popular without being populist – is not only possible: it is already flourishing. Zer0 is convinced that in the unthinking, blandly consensual culture in which we live, critical and engaged theoretical reflection is more important than ever before.

If you have enjoyed this book, why not tell other readers by posting a review on your preferred book site.

Recent bestsellers from Zero Books are:

In the Dust of This Planet
Horror of Philosophy vol. 1
Eugene Thacker
In the first of a series of three books on the Horror of
Philosophy, *In the Dust of This Planet* offers the genre of horror
as a way of thinking about the unthinkable.
Paperback: 978-1-84694-676-9 ebook: 978-1-78099-010-1

Capitalist Realism
Is there no alternative?
Mark Fisher
An analysis of the ways in which capitalism has presented itself
as the only realistic political-economic system.
Paperback: 978-1-84694-317-1 ebook: 978-1-78099-734-6

Rebel Rebel
Chris O'Leary
David Bowie: every single song. Everything you want to know,
everything you didn't know.
Paperback: 978-1-78099-244-0 ebook: 978-1-78099-713-1

Cartographies of the Absolute
Alberto Toscano, Jeff Kinkle
An aesthetics of the economy for the twenty-first century.
Paperback: 978-1-78099-275-4 ebook: 978-1-78279-973-3

Malign Velocities
Accelerationism and Capitalism
Benjamin Noys
Long listed for the Bread and Roses Prize 2015, *Malign
Velocities* argues against the need for speed, tracking
acceleration as the symptom of the ongoing crises of capitalism.
Paperback: 978-1-78279-300-7 ebook: 978-1-78279-299-4

Meat Market
Female Flesh under Capitalism
Laurie Penny
A feminist dissection of women's bodies as the fleshy fulcrum
of capitalist cannibalism, whereby women are both consumers
and consumed.
Paperback: 978-1-84694-521-2 ebook: 978-1-84694-782-7

Poor but Sexy
Culture Clashes in Europe East and West
Agata Pyzik
How the East stayed East and the West stayed West.
Paperback: 978-1-78099-394-2 ebook: 978-1-78099-395-9

Romeo and Juliet in Palestine
Teaching Under Occupation
Tom Sperlinger
Life in the West Bank, the nature of pedagogy and the role of a
university under occupation.
Paperback: 978-1-78279-637-4 ebook: 978-1-78279-636-7

Sweetening the Pill
or How We Got Hooked on Hormonal Birth Control
Holly Grigg-Spall
Has contraception liberated or oppressed women? *Sweetening*
the Pill breaks the silence on the dark side of hormonal
contraception.
Paperback: 978-1-78099-607-3 ebook: 978-1-78099-608-0

Readers of ebooks can buy or view any of these bestsellers by
clicking on the live link in the title. Most titles are published
in paperback and as an ebook. Paperbacks are available in
traditional bookshops. Both print and ebook formats are
available online.

Find more titles and sign up to our readers' newsletter
at http://www.johnhuntpublishing.com/culture-and-politics

Follow us on Facebook
at https://www.facebook.com/ZeroBooks
and Twitter at https://twitter.com/Zer0Books